Models of Metropolitan Ministry

B. Carlisle Driggers/Compiler

Broadman Press
Nashville, Tennessee

To

Mack M. Goss

Retired

Winston-Salem, North Carolina

And

Hoyt Blackwell

President Emeritus

Mars Hill College

Mars Hill, North Carolina

Model Ministers of the Gospel for Me

Contents

Introduction

January 1, 1977, William B. Tanner, president of Oklahoma Baptist University, Shawnee, Oklahoma, became the Executive Director-Treasurer of the Home Mission Board, Southern Baptist Convention. By design he spent the greatest portion of his time over the next two years reviewing firsthand the problems and opportunities of missions in America. He traveled extensively, attended training conferences, read futuristic materials, listened to pastors, laypersons, denominational leaders, seminary professors, and governmental officials, and visited churches and mission stations in all kinds of locations. One of Tanner's first conclusions following his research campaign was "We are in danger of losing our cities. If we do, we will lose the nation." He's right. Almost three-fourths of our citizens reside in metropolitan communities. The power base for government and economics is located in the cities and most of our people earn their living there. Yet, as is well known, our cities are in real trouble with many of them existing on the edge of bankruptcy. He also said, "God will hold us accountable for the stewardship of our vision." Again he is right. At this point two Biblical statements speak clearly and directly: "If my people, which are called by my name, shall humble themselves, and pray, and seek my face, and turn from their wicked ways; then will I hear from heaven, and will forgive their sin, and will heal their land" (2 Chron. 7:14). "Where there is no vision, the people perish" (Prov. 29:18).

This book is designed to increase our vision and our hope for the urban centers in the United States and to offer some possibilities for a positive, pragmatic approach to a healthy ministry. It is a compilation of case studies of twenty churches from across the United States which are located in transitional communities. The papers were written by ministers of these churches with assistance from some lay members.

Any greater metropolitan community breaks down into four basic areas: central city, inner city, the suburbs, and the rural-urban fringe. The twenty churches presented are located in one of those four areas, with five churches representing each area.

Metropolis continues to be in transition. Since relaxation of immigration laws in 1965, people from nations all over the world have poured into the United States. The flow has moved from a trickle to a flood of newcomers; and over 70 percent of them go directly to the cities, seeking jobs and housing. They are settling in central city and inner city neighborhoods. By 1990 there will be more Hispanics in America than blacks, with the majority locating in the cities. The same is true for Asians who, by A.D. 2000, will outnumber blacks in the nation.

For the first time since World War II, the black population within the nation's cities is not growing. The Census Bureau reports the number of blacks living in the suburbs, on the other hand, has grown by 34 percent since 1970. Blacks are moving to the suburbs at a rate of 5.2 percent to 1.4 percent for whites. At the same time, white flight from within the cities has practically stopped and young white college graduates are buying homes and renting apartments inside the cities. Exurbia also is realizing rapid change as small towns and open country areas on the rural-urban fringe are being invaded by new homeowners, mostly white. With spiraling gasoline prices and tax assessments, who knows what the future will bring to the cities and their surrounding communities.

In such a swirl, where are the churches? Many in central and inner city neighborhoods have relocated or merged or become introverted. Some suburban churches are maintaining the status quo, while a host of those on the rural-urban fringe are ignoring new residents. But there are hundreds of churches from central city to exurbia demonstrating compassionate, authentic approaches to ministry in their changing communities. The twenty churches in this book are those kinds of churches. Some of them have been at it for a long time while others are just beginning. One or two retreated a few years ago in the face of radical social change and are now in the process of regrouping to face new horizons.

One of the most difficult tasks in compiling this book was in selecting the churches to be included. Many outstanding churches in metropolitan centers were discovered, and most of them are going about their work without special recognition or fanfare. They simply are serving people, helping the country, and loving God.

The twenty case studies are offered as examples of what can be done if pastors, the laity, and denominational leaders are willing. The churches are not perfect by any means, and they would be the first to admit it; but they are trying to be faithful to the call of their Lord, to walk in his footsteps. They can serve as means of comparison for other churches in similar circumstances.

A number of people recommended churches for these case studies, and I appreciate their guidance: Jack O'Neal, California; Ezra Earl Jones, Ohio; William B. Rogers, Kentucky; Harold E. Scott, Pennsylvania; James Nelson and Don Hammer, Georgia; Phil Rodgerson, Virginia; Jere Allen, Alabama; Ernest Mehaffey, South Carolina; John C. DeBoer, New York, and many others.

I also am indebted to those individuals who helped me work on the case study papers in preparation for printing. My colleagues, Emmanuel L. McCall, Edward L. Wheeler, Elaine Furlow, and Celeste Loucks were of real assistance along with my English-teacher wife, Jeanette. It is doubtful that this project would have been completed at all without the patience, organizational ability, and typing skills of my secretary, Bonnie Hancock.

It is my prayer that these twenty case studies will be of considerable usefulness to pastors, lay persons, seminary instructors, students, and denominational workers. There are many excellent, innovative ideas for metropolitan ministry discussed on these pages along with proven, tested concepts.

I sincerely hope we can be good stewards of the vision God grants us—that we may be on mission in urban areas.

B. Carlisle Driggers

Atlanta, Georgia
January, 1979

I
Central City Churches

1.
First Baptist Church
Albuquerque, New Mexico
Morris H. Chapman, Pastor

Morris Chapman is a graduate of Mississippi College, Clinton, Mississippi. He also studied at Southwestern Baptist Theological Seminary, Fort Worth, Texas, where he earned the Master of Divinity and Doctor of Ministry degrees. While attending seminary, he was the recipient of the Stella P. Ross Memorial Award in Evangelism. In addition to his responsibilities as a pastor, he is the Chaplain of the University of New Mexico basketball team. Betty Danielson, historian of the church, assisted in preparing the case study.

With its gambling houses, bars and street shootouts, in the 1800s, Albuquerque, N.M., looked like a wild west town straight out of a Gunsmoke backdrop.

En route to California for the gold rush, evangelical preacher Hiram Walter Reed and his family stopped off in New Mexico. The military governor implored Reed to stay, "due to the spiritual darkness of the people." By October, 1853, First Baptist Church, Albuquerque began in an adobe building in what is now "Old Town." Hiram Reed was the pastor.

The church was temporarily interrupted by the Civil War and for several years met in lodges and rented rooms. For awhile, progress was slow and frustrating. One pastor wrote: "The extreme difficulty of this work cannot be fully comprehended by anyone who has not been on the field." Wrote another, "I feel that I am preaching to a passing procession. Persons whom I have baptized since coming here are scattered from Chicago to the Pacific Ocean."

When First Baptist began, it ministered to a town bustling with fifteen hundred persons! Yet, by the 1950s, Sunday School averaged twelve hundred weekly. The church, located in downtown Albuquerque, now reflects the ethnic diversity of the state and has a strong emphasis on ministry and missions.

First Church began its first mission in 1905. Since that time, the church has fostered nine missions with thirty-two churches being planted eventually.

Currently, the city population includes: 52 percent Anglo; 37 percent Hispanic; 7 percent Indian; 3 percent black, and 1 percent Oriental/Church growth experts may believe a truly cosmopolitan church cannot flourish. Yet, this church has proven to be an exception. First Baptist Church, Albuquerque has warmly received persons of all colors, races, and cultures. During a recent visit, Dr. W. R. Estep, professor of church history at Southwestern Baptist Theological Seminary said, "This is one of the most cosmopolitan churches I know. In fact, next to Spurgeon's Tabernacle in London, I think there is no church of my acquaintance that has reached out into so many ethnic groups with the gospel of Jesus Christ."

First Church began an Indian mission in 1923 which grew to be a full-scale work and has been operated by our Home Mission Board since 1931. In 1953, a Jewish woman who had escaped Nazi persecution during World War II, was baptized into our church. In 1959, a Jewish man and a Chinese man became Christians and entered the baptismal waters together.

In 1962, the church sponsored a Cuban family and began our international ministry. English classes started in the home of this Cuban family. Later fourteen other Cuban refugees participated in the English classes which are conducted in the main building now. This ministry has expanded during the past fifteen years to include English classes for university graduate students, their wives and mothers, wives of U.S. servicemen, refugees from Vietnam, Laos and Cambodia, and local Spanish-speaking Americans and Mexicans. Our church has ministered to more than six hundred internationals representing fifty-six countries of the world.

During the early years, teachers were trained through workshops conducted by Pauline Cammack and Mildred Blankenship. Our leaders also participated in the special sessions offered by the Home Mission Board at Glorieta Baptist Conference Center in New Mexico. Scriptures and prayers are part of every English-teaching session, and with two exceptions, each person has been interested in learning about Christianity.

In 1967, a Bible study class for internationals became a part of our regular Church Training curriculum. In 1969, need for more Bible study led to the establishment of an international Sunday School department. Bilingual New Testaments, pictorial New Testaments, and *The Story of Jesus* by Dr. Frank Laubach, are teaching tools. Simplified quarterlies were added to the curriculum. Our church now has members from Cuba, Hong Kong, Korea, Laos, Mexico, Nicaragua, Okinawa, Philippines, Singapore, Taiwan, Thailand, and Vietnam. Entire families of internationals have become Christians and members of our church. Some are U.S. citizens and many are proud and successful business owners.

In September 1975, a Vietnamese wedding took place in our sanctuary. The bride was a descendant of Vietnamese royalty and a convert of Southern Baptist missionaries; the groom, won to Christ, and baptized into our church. The wedding was performed in both English and Vietnamese. Since then we have had numerous international weddings.

Picnics in the mountains and parks, potluck suppers, showers for brides and mothers-to-be, Thanksgiving dinners, Christmas parties in our homes, Chinese New Year celebrations and Valentine banquets—all are a part of our international ministry. One Chinese lady expressed her appreciation for this ministry:

> At my age, on this foreign land, I started to learn English from you. Kindly, you take me to every class which I've so enjoyed. Never asking for any rewards, you teach me our Lord's words. As the warm breeze of spring, his love has brought hope to every corner of the world. All of us can belong to the family of God—you make me convinced so. Your kindness, your consideration, your help, all of your charms, are bestowed by the Lord. This land, full of his love, is no longer foreign to me.

Currently, the international ministry involves ten to twelve teachers meeting with twenty-five to forty students for two hours, twice a week; for classes in English as a second language; and a Sunday School department with an attendance of forty to sixty students with ten teachers leading in Bible study.

In 1977, God sent the John Tusiri family to us. They were former residents of Thailand where John was a successful and prosperous businessman, Christian leader, and lay minister. The Tusiris established themselves in business and became active members of our church. John often confided that he longed for the Lord to call him into full-time ministry. Soon he responded to the ministry among our rapidly growing Oriental population. With the help of state missions and the Home Mission Board, the ministry was launched in January 1978. He became the mission pastor. This mission operates closely with our international ministry. Worship services are conducted in Chinese on Sunday mornings, and in Thai on Sunday afternoons. More than fifty persons now attend Chinese services regularly which are translated into two additional Chinese dialects. Chinese, Thai, and other Orientals mingle during a meal scheduled between the close of the Chinese services and the beginning of the services in Thai. We plan to provide transportation and child care facilities to enable increased participation in these programs.

In 1963, the first black family united with the church. Some opposition resulted and a few families left. Yet, now, more than a score of blacks are integral parts of our fellowship. That first family is still with us.

Our Sunday School is staffed by all races, colors, and cultures of people. The bonds of Christian love are stronger than ever as we serve together.

Our church also has pioneered in work with single adults. In 1956 we founded the annual single adult retreat at Glorieta which since has grown into an additional conference at Ridgecrest Baptist Conference Center in North Carolina.

Between 1950 to 1960 First Baptist Church felt a sharp decline in membership as 1,025 members changed their letters to newly organized churches. For example, in 1960, 432 members formed the base for the new Sandia Baptist Church. This pattern of loss in membership turned around, however, in 1971, with a vastly expanded bus ministry. Total Sunday School and worship service attendance increased as fourteen buses brought an average of approximately five hundred persons to Sunday morning Bible study. However, the church members and leaders were unprepared to care for so many new children and youth. In April, 1974, when I became the pastor, I encouraged the church to gradually de-emphasize (not discontinue) the bus ministry. We reemphasized and expanded efforts to reach entire families, especially young adults. Now, the church is enjoying a substantial period of growth and is recommitted to remaining downtown.

In 1959, after several years of decline in the downtown area, the church purchased a large parcel of land miles away from the downtown area as a possible future building site. At the old downtown location, property immediately surrounding the main buildings was totally unavailable. The church seemed to be hemmed in, and was continuing in the way of so many other declining downtown churches. However, after much effort in long-range planning, serious deliberations and seasons of prayer, the church came to the point of recommitting herself to remaining in the center of the downtown area. Through an Urban Renewal Project the property around our existing church was made available to us at a phenomenally affordable price. It was as though God had kept his hand on this property until such time as we were willing and able to utilize it for his glory. The nineteen and one-half acres away from the downtown area were sold for more than enough to purchase the adjoining property downtown.

With the recommitment of the church to remain in the downtown area, my own strategy for attracting entire families, especially young adult families has involved the following:

1. Worship services that are flexible and spontaneous; simple gospel preaching which presents the basics of the Bible with relevance and fervor.

2. A dynamic music ministry which involves all ages and centers on celebration and victory.

3. A contagious atmosphere which says, "if you are absent, you will miss something wonderful."

4. Creating a sense of expectancy that individuals will respond

to the love of Christ during each worship service.

5. A consistent emphasis on outreach and evangelism.

I developed and led a witnessing training course, which we named, "The King's Command." The course met twice weekly for ten to thirteen weeks. An hour and a half was spent learning the basics of witnessing. Another hour and a half weekly was devoted to participating in outreach and witnessing visitation. Inexperienced visitors were teamed with experienced ones. Some 150 people have completed the course. On visitation nights, and throughout the week, scores of teachers, deacons, choir members, and class members go out seeking to enlist prospects in the church. They visit in regions of the city nearest their homes in order to save time in travel. More and more of our people are recognizing that outreach visitation and witnessing is a divine imperative!

6. Establish a strong rapport with the deacons of the church, based upon a trusting, caring, serving concept.

7. Fully utilize the abilities and interests of the members in the teaching, training, and service organizations of the church. I've always believed that "as goes the Sunday School, so goes the church!"

When my family and I arrived on the scene, we found a Young Adult Sunday School Department without leadership and not enough young adult members for even one class. My wife, Jodi, accepted the position as Director of the Young Adult Department. Employing tried and proven methods of Sunday School growth (strong Bible teaching; teachers and leaders who care about people; small conversational-group size classes; aggressive outreach and ministry visitation; beginning new classes as soon as the potential is evident; using class organizations which involve more people in the work and ministry of the class; and providing meaningful social and fellowship activities), the "less than one class" of young adults has now grown into an entire Young Adult Division with four departments, twelve classes, an enrollment of 216, and an average attendance of 115. And they've only begun to grow!

8. Develop a quality television ministry.

First Baptist first began broadcasting its services on radio in 1930. In 1954, and for the next two years, the morning worship services were televised. We continue to broadcast our morning worship services on radio, but our use of television has been of an entirely different nature. With the help of professionals, a series of television "commercials" have been prepared and shown during prime time slots. These spots are always tied in, tactically, with a current and simultaneous emphasis in the church. Over the last five years both thirty-second and sixty-second spots have been taped for television. We found that nightly newscasts at six o'clock and ten o'clock drew the greatest response. Special events, especially ball games of heightened interest in the community, are also good for church spots.

The first series of television commercials were of an introductory nature, introducing the church to the city. The viewer was always issued a general invitation to visit with us. However, this invitation was later defined more clearly by inviting the viewer to hear the pastor preach Sunday morning on a particular subject. These highly polished spots proved to be a statement of purpose to the people of our city. They came to realize that things were happening at "old First Church." Our television ministry has evolved from trying to create *awareness* to trying to create *action* on the part of the viewer, helping him understand that Jesus cares. Always, the television spots have been of the nature to offer support and benefit to churches all over New Mexico and of all denominations.

9. Establish a high profile.

Through community work all over the city, plus our radio and television ministries, First Baptist is now well-known. My service as chaplain of the university basketball team has helped.

10. The production of quality printed materials.

11. Build a staff of competent, creative people.

The importance of personnel cannot be overstated. Men and women uniquely gifted to achieve certain goals within the context of the church's needs must be enlisted. We have worked hard to have an excellent staff.

12. Constructing modern education facilities.

The image projected by our buildings and surrounding structures in the downtown area was insufficient to demonstrate the vibrant and exciting ministry taking place in the church. Ultimately, four major buildings, including one five-story building, have been demolished. Two purposes were accomplished. (1) Room was made available for new construction plus a five hundred-car paved, lighted, and landscaped parking area. (2) A feeling of spaciousness was created, making the entire area more appealing.

Our beautiful educational facilities complete with landscaped courtyard now speak volumes about the church and her growing ministries. The new fifty thousand square foot facility is located on two city blocks. An additional and adjoining thirty-five thousand square feet of space has been remodeled providing adequate space for church offices, two senior adult departments, the international department, two median adult departments, five youth departments, and other support facilities. A third building, known as "The Central Place" is one block away from the main buildings. This recently remodeled facility provides beautiful space for indoor recreation and meeting places for single adults and the Oriental Mission.

A little more than three years ago the church entered into a "Together We Build" building fund campaign and, as a result, secured pledges for more than one million dollars. To date, these pledges have been approximately 90 percent received.

As the magnificent new facilities were being occupied, a greatly expanded teaching, reaching, and training organization was projected which called for more than one hundred additional Sunday School workers. When the time came, more than enough workers were enlisted to staff the enlarged organization. As a result, growth has accelerated, more people have been reached and ministered to, workers are basking in the satisfaction of having a part in something significant and successful, and more people are being won to Christ and added to the church.

Other indicators of God's blessings upon this downtown missionary and evangelistic church include the following:

- More and more of our youth are responding to God's call to the full-time gospel ministry and to other church-related vocations.
- During the past two years, four couples have gone from our

fellowship to the mission fields of Venezuela, Brazil, Zambia, and Europe.
- Gifts to missionary causes, local, national, and foreign, continue to increase significantly.
- Faithful members and leaders attend First Baptist Church from as far as seventy miles away.

Persons are coming from all over the Albuquerque metropolitan area in order to express and demonstrate their concern for the central city. During the past several years of suburban development, thousands of families have fled the deteriorating, depressive, and perplexing inner-city with all its unpleasant sounds, sights, and smells, supposedly to find a pleasant refuge. While many of our members now live in such fine areas, their hearts and concerns remain where the needs exist. Here they have a hand in communicating God's love through Bible study, equipping and training, Christian education, children's work, child care, youth programs, outreach, discipleship, share groups, home Bible study, special education, family seminars, summer youth camps, Vacation Bible Schools, Backyard Bible clubs, Christian social ministries (convalescent centers, rescue missions, with transients and migrants), in addition to work with nationals and internationals of every known race, culture, and economic strata.

Where else can one find so much satisfaction and so many opportunities for Christian service, growth and development than in the city?

In very definite ways our plans for the immediate future are fixed. They involve the expansion and improvement of every program and ministry now carried on by First Baptist Church. The church staff has involved the deacons, church council, Sunday School council, other church program leadership, as well as the various segments of church membership in developing a short-term program of growth. The theme of this plan is "One Step Beyond" and the scriptural basis is Colossians 2:6-7: "As ye have therefore received Christ Jesus the Lord, so walk ye in him: Rooted and built up in him, and stablished in the faith, as ye have been taught, abounding therein with thanksgiving." Some of the features of the program will include a prospect banquet, enlisting additional teachers for Sunday School, debt retirement, and a Family Life Enrichment Conference.

We have developed also a set of long-range goals which include:

1. The rapid retirement of our church indebtedness to the point where we can erect a Church Worship Center which will further enhance our "Architectural Master Plan" in the heart of downtown Albuquerque.

2. The establishment of a vastly expanded benevolent-type ministry designed to lift the level of economically deprived individuals and families who seem to be an increasingly larger part of the downtown area.

3. The establishment and the erection of a building for a Family Life Recreation Center which will be designed to provide a place for Christian recreation and social life for persons of all races, nationalities, and cultures.

4. A statewide weekly television ministry.

Other long-range plans include the continual expansion and development of existing ministries and mission activities.

I try to challenge our people to follow the dreams and visions we had as we began our journey as pastor and people. Some skeptics said it couldn't be done. Yet, this congregation of God's people has refused to surrender in defeat. Perhaps we can understand why some said it couldn't be done. After all, people have predicted that "downtown" in the cities of America will never regain popularity or economic strength, but Albuquerque is resisting that attitude. The citizens of our city have not given up on "downtown," and I am grateful to be able to state that First Baptist Church is emerging as one of the spiritual leaders for our greater metropolitan community.

2.
New Shiloh Baptist Church
Baltimore, Maryland
Harold A. Carter, Pastor

The Reverend Dr. Harold Carter was born in Selma, Alabama. He graduated from Alabama State College and Crozer Theological Seminary, Chester, Pennsylvania. He also holds the Doctor of Ministry degree from Colgate-Rochester Divinity School and the Doctor of Philosophy degree from Saint Mary's Seminary, Baltimore, Maryland. From 1959 to 1964 he was the pastor of Court Street Baptist Church in Lynchburg, Virginia, one of America's oldest black Baptist congregations. He is married and has two children.

New Shiloh Church has refused to settle for a ministry that raises salaries of the personnel, pays all bills and keeps everyone satisfied. It has rather sought to translate productive soil into creative growth.

This congregation of over three thousand members was organized in 1901 by Rev. W. W. Allen. He was characterized as a man large in both stature and faith. His initial congregation numbered two people but during his ministry the two multiplied to more than three thousand. From the beginning a strong evangelistic emphasis was at work. This fact was reflected on the third Sunday of August, 1928, when more than three hundred persons were baptized in the swimming pool at Druid Hill Park.

After Allen's tenure, which exceeded forty years, Dr. J. Timothy Boddie came to the helm. He is an older brother to the beloved Charles Emerson Boddie, president of the American Baptist Theological Seminary, Nashville, Tennessee. Boddie's expertise lay in organization, and he did a masterful job of bringing discipline and coordination to this mass gathering of folk. He led a different kind of transition—that of helping a people who had been called together by a fervent shout to become a people better aware and more articulate of what they were shouting about.

But as often happens, masses diminish in the arduous task of discipline. The crowds of three thousand during Allen's pastorate diminished to about twelve hundred by the end of Boddie's twenty years. A powerful preacher, an uncompromising leader, Boddie left a solid foundation upon which his successor could build. I became the third pastor of New Shiloh in 1964 at the age of twenty-eight. We are affiliated with the American Baptist Convention, U.S.A., and also the Progressive National Baptist Convention.

New Shiloh is strategically located in downtown Baltimore on the corner of Fremont Avenue and Lanvale Street. It is surrounded by all of the advantages and disadvantages of an urban church. There are the stable citizens who have lived for many years in their well-appointed marble-step row homes. There are the tenants who worked and made money, but carelessly threw salaries and lives away. There are community alcoholics and general drifters.

This community has claimed the lives of thousands who migrated from the deep south and other rural communities seeking a better life. They left behind the triangular support that their southern roots had provided: community identity; the extended family of uncles, aunts, cousins, kinfolk; and the nurturing church.

In the new setting their children were born into a world with no viable family or community support. The press of people meant that the local banker, preacher, teacher, or sheriff did not know the "average Joe" as he would have "down home." In this uprooted condition, thousands of black persons developed frustrations, lost a sense of hope and a desire for the better things of life. Tenement houses were often neglected, communities lost their beauty, neighborhood bars became familiar meeting places. These conditions provided the festering ground for the long summers of discontent during the sixties.

Into this condition came the prophetic voice and leadership of Martin Luther King, Jr. His ministry of nonviolence, based upon the teachings of Jesus Christ, did more than any other single person to prove to me that the church could provide a vital difference in the quality of urban life.

The civil rights struggles of the sixties were led largely by youth. The parents of black sons and daughters were delighted to see them seek a new social order. Many felt that the church had failed the youth. Others felt that ministers were the voices of downtown power structures. Many became disillusioned with the church. Some just dropped out. Others opted for new and strange religions.

I tried to approach this problem with three principles:

1. A relevant sermon to adults must be relevant to youth and vice versa.

2. A relevant worship to adults must be relevant to youth.

3. Relevant involvement of youth in the church must challenge them as disciples of Christ now and not as a future generation consigned to wait on the death of their elders.

It was not long before hundreds of young people were joining the church, involving themselves in its ministry. This happened because youth were not singled out as a group to be catered to, but as those in need of the saving grace of Jesus Christ.

Getting people in church is one thing, getting them active is quite another. Previously, New Shiloh was organized around the traditional concept of deacons, trustees, and a board of Christian education that coordinated all mission and educational matters. While the 11:00 A.M. worship service overflowed the one thousand seat auditorium, Sunday church school barely had two hundred. The Friday night prayer service drew only a faithful few.

I was convinced that the study of the Bible and a directed growth in prayer and praise would make a difference. We began a Saturday "neighborhood youth hour." Youth leaders, including a youthful associate minister, were selected. Innovative ministries began attracting numbers of young people. This activity developed in 1972 into our Saturday Church School. At the beginning this was a novel experience—at least 946 persons participated. The novelty has worn off, but an average of four hundred are still reached.

Each January, we hold two workshops to plan the year's church program. Each church department shares its intentions. The Saturday Church School concept was formalized during these workshops and the following guidelines were adopted:

1. That the church school meet each Saturday from 10:00 A.M. until 1:00 P.M.

2. That church school studies become more biblically centered and that an editorial staff augment the literature.

3. That Bible training be supplemented by offering professional training in reading, English, mathematics, music, arts and crafts, cooking, and some sports.

4. Professionally trained people in the church were challenged to commit themselves to the demands of such an innovative program.

5. The spirit of evangelism was to be kept alive in the church school using creative special events.

The schedule recommended was:

10:00 A.M. First class period—devotions in all rooms with general churchwide Bible study.

11:15 A.M. General creative worship hour (a trained worship committee plans all services).

12:00 NOON Elective period (one hour).

This has been a very successful venture. It elicited a dedication from many people that would not have been possible under the old system. Adults and parents have made commitments to basic Bible study. The pastor's community Bible class, averaging seventy-five adults, has given me the chance to implant deeper mission and evangelical Christian doctrines.

The "youth express class" has been conducted by adults having special skills in counseling and a deep Christian commitment.

People have been won to Christ through our Saturday Church School. To see members winning others to Christ and serving the needs of humanity is both necessary and demanding. Not to seek that goal is to permit the local church to settle into a lethargy that usually destroys what life it possesses. Worship must be translated into Christian actions. There cannot be a total separation between worship as witness and work, and community deeds as witness and work.

Thus, New Shiloh claims Christianity as primarily a mystical religion whose faith transforms the lives of people. Before any church can be strong in Christian evangelism, a sense of the mysterious power of God must be working in the lives of the believers. We must refuse to believe that a social gospel that argues for man to order his own society through legislation and community actions is somehow more relevant than the fundamental message of the gospel declaring, "You must be born again."

All members of New Shiloh are motivated toward Christian evangelism and missions. The formal organization of that came in 1972. Previously the church had used the usual methods of evangelism and witness. It had a missionary society of predominantly faithful women, a conference with neighboring churches on evangelism, at least two full week revivals each year with the pastor preaching one of them. Still there was the feeling of being rutted in tradition.

The first change was to disband the missionary society as a separate group. The entire church was then organized around the concepts of evangelism and missions. All auxiliary and department leaders attended several Saturday morning workshops and out of those meetings came these commitments:

1. Every member should win persons to Christ and assist others in spiritual and temporal need.

2. All auxiliaries must provide a specific evangelistic or mission purpose, and openly state those plans for approval by the church.

3. Thursday after each first Sunday of the month was set aside for missionary crusade night, during which the entire church would report progress.

Consequently, these actions have resulted from the redirection of purpose:

1. Groups and auxiliaries were challenged to equip men and women for service instead of just hearing sick reports, receiving dues, or seeking a reason for being.

2. A weekly program of food evangelism was instituted. A huge pantry box was placed in the vestibule to receive food gifts. The young adults who are responsible for this minister to more than five hundred families yearly, not only meeting physical needs but witnessing. Thanksgiving and Christmas are no longer the only times Christian love is expressed.

3. The church is regularly involved in ministries with homes for senior adults, detention centers, and penal institutions. These ministries include worship services, counseling, rehabilitation services,

family support, and evangelistic witness. The "Sons of the Prophet" (other ministers in the church) are used extensively in these ministries.

4. The men provide transportation for members on mission as well as to the church house. They serve as disciples for the Saturday Church School program. As such, they gather new persons in their communities who need the services of the church and see to their development. They guide the churchwide prayer-breakfast averaging three hundred persons on the Saturday before the third Sunday in each month. They organize the "family solidarity parades" which involve more than two thousand persons. The community in a two-mile radius of the church observes the police escorted parade with such signs as:

No Generation Gap in Christian Family!

Mother and Father, Sons and Daughters, Together!

The Bible, the Key to Family Living!

Both television and newspapers cover the parade.

5. Radio and prayer ministries: New Shiloh broadcasts on two AM stations in Baltimore and one station in Alabama. Two telephone prayer lines with recorded prayer and meditation are available. These are not supported by the public but by the church budget and cooperating radio stations. These ministries continue to provide new opportunities for mission and witness.

6. One night crusades: The radio and prayer ministries help spur effective one night crusades, where all families of the church are called to worship. Each member has been charged with the responsibility of bringing the unsaved and unchurched. The entire music department is involved. The pastor or other ministers preach. The results have been phenomenal—

Respect for weekday services has heightened.

Persons limited by Sunday involvements are free to attend.

Radio and prayer ministries call persons to come during weeknights as well as on Sundays.

Youth night crusades on Saturday have drawn more than three hundred looking for something to do or somewhere to go.

7. All family recognition services, with certificates presented for

family participation, has also strengthened the witness and ministry of the church.

8. Sons of the Prophet: Eighteen persons from New Shiloh have announced their callings to full-time Christian service since 1965. Nine of them are now pastors of strong churches. All of them have or are completing theological training. One of them, Brenda Greene, is a full-time minister of Christian Education, as is our minister at large, Rev. Vincent Thompson.

9. New Shiloh sponsored an evangelistic crusade at the Baltimore civic center in 1978 with thirteen thousand present.

10. The New Shiloh women held a prayer retreat in Baltimore's Hilton Hotel which drew more than one thousand prayer partners. Another such meeting brought prayer partners including Jews, Gentiles, Muslims, Holiness, and South Africans.

New Shiloh is committed to being innovative, not for the sake of gimmickry, but always seeking to discover where and how God can best be served. The church will continue those programs that are relevant, discard irrelevant ones, and seek other means for proclaiming the gospel of Jesus Christ.

One of those ways may be television. Giving a witness in this international city must not be diminished. New Shiloh has been involved in evangelistic endeavors with other church bodies such as the city wide Easter worship in Memorial Stadium. Usually twenty thousand attend. Even organized church travel to the Holy Land has strengthened the resolve and enlarged the visions of New Shiloh's members.

These reflections summarize the principles guiding our people:

1. A local church is not made powerful or strong by the pastor attending all events and keeping up with every need. What really helps the people is the vision and directives the pastor provides.

2. New Shiloh has been spiritually energized by moving away from customary practices and trying to follow new leadings of the Spirit.

3. No urban church can effectively reach masses of people behind its walls.

4. Prayer must be recognized as a mighty force with God to

unite and undergird the total involvement of Christian ministry. The altar prayer after the sermon gives a convenient opportunity for everyone to make some specific commitment to the directed content of the message.

5. The preaching of the gospel must never be replaced. It has been the major avenue in molding the people of New Shiloh, gradually causing them to think larger than themselves.

6. The entire church must be mobilized if evangelism and mission efforts are to succeed.

7. The strength of the Christian family is a mighty force, making possible an effective ministry among the people.

8. The prominence of the minister's family and Christian teamwork between pastor and wife help to provide a foundation for witness beyond the pulpit and ecclesiastical bounds.

I have no desire to be known as strictly a "black preacher" or a "seminary preacher" or by any other restrictive title. I only want to be a preacher for the Lord Jesus Christ to be used in any setting among any people. To me the church has always been greater than the parish I served. At New Shiloh we are committed to being "A Church Beyond the Deadening Ruts—Determined to Live with Christ."

3.

Luther Place Memorial Church Washington, D.C. John F. Steinbruck, Pastor

Rev. John Steinbruck has been the senior minister at Luther Place Memorial Church since 1970. He earned his Bachelor of Science degree at the University of Pennsylvania and his Master of Divinity at the Lutheran Theological Seminary in Philadelphia. In 1976 Daniel Payne College conferred on him the Doctor of Divinity degree in recognition of his contributions to interracial and interfaith understanding and cooperation. He is married and has five children.

The streets of a city are always an interesting study . . . and especially so when they converge at a major metropolitan intersection and enable an interflow of people from every sector, station, and place of origin. Such a configuration exists at Thomas Circle, Washington, D.C.

Luther Place Memorial Church lives in the midst of this swirl. For more than a century this memorial, dedicated to peace and freedom shortly after the close of the War Between the States, has stood as a convenient symbol of Lutheranism's presence in the Nation's capital city. Its red-sandstone structure of European-style architecture forms a backdrop for the statue of Martin Luther, which faces south on Vermont Avenue toward the White House only a few blocks away. Luther Place has provided a forum for prominent pastors—some have served as chaplain to House and Senate of the U.S. Congress, have taught in colleges and seminaries, have given administrative leadership to the parent Lutheran Church in America, and/or have gone on to fame as did former pastor, Lloyd C. Douglas, author of religious novels, such as *The Robe* and *The Magnificent Obsession.*

Beginning in the 1950s the restful history of this church came to an end. Suburbs were developing rapidly, enticing residents from a crowded and turbulent city. The black liberation movement was beginning, often turning Washington into a focal point where the struggle was dramatized for all the nation and world to see. In the 1960s this movement merged its turbulence with the heightening resistance to the Vietnamese War, sparking a counterculture revolution. Luther Place was frequently enveloped by protest demonstrations bringing an atmosphere of fire and smoke, tear gas, police, National Guard, Marines, and armored cars, ultimately leaving in their wake a void to be filled by urban migrants, street hustlers, drug pushers and addicts, prostitutes and pimps—mixing with tourists, commuters, churchgoers, and neighborhood residents.

Throughout this period and into the present the neighborhood has been and is a collage of "the good, the bad, and the ugly." Along with the remains of charred and closed buildings stand institutional monuments, such as the offices of the National Education Association, the National Geographic Society, the National Rifle Association, the Washington *Post*, together with posh hotels, embassies, restaurants, and concrete parking lots.

Slipping between the cracks of Washington's high-powered structures are the urban migrants of every sort. Sometimes known as "street people," they range from the homeless alcoholics to the youthful wanderers in hiking shoes and wearing backpacks. Also included are the "shopping-cart ladies" who live hand-to-mouth, and sleep on park benches or on steam grates of office buildings, and the newly-arrived husbands and fathers from West Virginia or South Carolina in search of work to support a distant family. Mixed in with these groups is an assortment of visitors—from tourists who come from everywhere on earth to demonstrators advocating every conceivable cause. At all hours, including 11:00 Sunday morning, hundreds of prostitutes encircle Luther Place, hustling the "johns," cruising by morning, noon, and night.

Our reaction to such a diversified situation came more by evolution than by revolution. Certainly such crises as the uprising after the assassination of Martin Luther King, Jr. and the antiwar demonstrations during the Vietnam years expedited the process. In April 1968 the congregation moved spontaneously to meet human needs by organizing to provide shelter, food, and clothing to victims of the burnings of Fourteenth, Seventh, and H Streets. Luther Place also recognized early the opportunity to relate to the counterculture movement. By the mid-1960s local talent such as Tony Taylor, Roberta Flack, and other professionals helped the church to establish the Iguana Coffee House and Sunday afternoon worship with jazz and other art forms. These efforts were widely publicized and enjoyed initial enthusiasm which waned as the Fourteenth Street corridor became a conduit for drug traffic infested with prostitutes and criminals.

The late 1960s and early 1970s were periods of testing for the congregation, both from without and within. With decentralization of government and the development of suburbs, membership declined significantly. Over a period of many months in 1970-72 the congregation agonized over its *raison d'etre* in that place at that time. The community of worshipers remaining were at least open and tolerant and, at best, willing to reach out and embrace the new age that had erupted with volcanic intensity all about it. While a significant number opted for suburban security and stability, a strong and dedicated remnant stayed to provide a viable core of communing members who were eager and willing to seize the time in God's name. The attitude seemed to be one of confidence in God's future even if that future should mean death for the congregation . . . claiming with St. Paul the assurance that nothing "will be able to separate us from the love of God in Christ Jesus our Lord" (Rom. 8:39, RSV).

In the struggle the congregation took advantage of the expertise of professional consultants (Lutheran and non-Lutheran) but found that only the local congregation can come to grips with specifics and plan to be at home in and with a community, sharing hospitality. In the end, the key to our situation appeared to be our space (thirty-seven thousand square feet) and its usage—dedicated to worship, education, service, and fellowship.

Time and again, we pondered the situation—both in large and small groups. To minister, we decided to enter into coalitions with diversified groups of concerned partners: Protestants, Jews, Catholics and even persons professing no religious affiliation. This arrangement has worked and is still working.

All of the Luther Place and its N Street Village ministries operate from an interreligious base that produces synergistic results not possible if attempted unilaterally as a single Lutheran congregation. Our church building and block of houses contiguous to the church include the full spread of Matthew 25: "I was hungry and you fed me, thirsty and you gave me a drink; I was a stranger and you received me in your homes, naked and you clothed me; I was sick and you took care of me, in prison and you visited me" (Matt. 25:35-36, TEV).

Every ministry has one to three full-time coordinators and hosts of volunteers who provide services (food, clothing, medical supplies, prescriptions)—Bread for the City; D.C. Hotline; Zacchaeus Medical Clinic; Deborah's Place—reinforced by resident hospices such as Cornerstone House; Zacchaeus House; Barabbas House; Bonhoeffer House; Isaiah House, and others in the making, on budgets that range from the level of $4,000 (Barabbas House); $8,000 (Bread for the City); to $18,000 (Zacchaeus Medical Clinic). No government funds are sought or received. Support comes from an increasingly wide base that includes individuals, churches, Air Force chaplains, some foundation help, and anonymous gifts. But the ability of Luther Place, the base congregation, to be supportively flexible in the flow and planned dispersion of its funds is the key to survival.

In a word, resourcefulness is crucial. When our village houses needed repair and restoration, volunteer Naval Reserve Seabees were invited, with all their skills in plumbing, electrical repair, masonry and carpentry, to work on Luther Place buildings. The savings were thousands upon thousands of dollars.

The bottom line is that, not only does two plus two add up synergistically to six or eight or ten, but Luther Place is the recipient of serendipitous blessings of new ministries that are discovered enroute.

This is our evangelism. The Hebrew concept is kiddush hashem —"to sanctify God's name by bearing witness in body, mind, soul, and spirit amidst the idolatries of the world to the difference that faith makes, even unto martyrdom."

By evangelism we mean to exemplify (not impose) the presence of God; and as such, to be a conduit of light into the world and to nations, even as Isaiah and Jesus envisioned and lived out.

Amidst incest, violence, and prostitution of every sort; amidst hunger and homelessness, wretchedness and decay, Luther Place has turned the corner statistically and is growing in the number of worshipers and working members. But that is not our goal. Primarily we are called to be faithful, not numerous!

Nor is our future assured. It is that truth that enables us to face our own death as a congregation, should faithfulness require that, even as we live every day in the midst of Washington's dead and dying.

The fact is, Luther Place cannot, dare not, and will not die when it is so critically needed in Washington, D.C. Where would God's people go? What would they call home? The White House? The NEA or the NRA? The Soviet embassy? The Washington *Post?* Justice Department? HEW? FBI? Holiday Inns? Garfinckel's Department Store? . . . Where?

Luther Place must be "that place." Simply a hospice. It is to be a shelter, an oasis, a refuge from the harsh environment.

Hospitality is the key to Luther Place's self-understanding and identity as a theological expression at the hub of Washington, D.C. As a concept, hospitality is acceptable and palatable to Luther Place. It is as American as apple pie, yet it has radical implications that are inexhaustible and ultimate.

To be hospitable is to convert the hostis into a hospes, the enemy into a guest. Hospitality is a relationship between host and guest with enough freedom that both can reveal their most precious gifts and bring new life to each other.[1] To accept hospitality is to open oneself to healing and shelter. As Henri J. M. Nouwen says in his book *Reaching Out:*

The German word for hospitality means, "friendship of the guest." The Dutch word means the freedom of the guest. Though it might show that the Dutch people find freedom more important than friendship it definitely shows that hospitality wants to offer friendship without binding the guest, and freedom without leaving him alone. Hospitality, therefore, means primarily the creation of a free space where the stranger can enter and become a friend instead of an enemy. Hospitality is not to change people, but to offer them space where change can take place.[2]

Luther Place strives to be a hospice, a non-threatening, non-hostile environment where people are called to change, but at the same time are accepted as they are. That there will always be a need for hospitality stems from the basic need of all people to be and to feel at home.

An article in the May 1976 issue of *The Catholic Worker*[3] says it well:

Like hospitality, being at home has less to do with a place, a geography, than it has to do with an attitude. In the Christian tradition, we are reminded of the pilgrimage we are on—but our hearts will only let us be pilgrims for a time, not forever. Many stories in the Gospels speak in terms of coming home: the woman accused of adultery, whom Jesus did not condemn to life-long uncertainty, was told to sin no more, and go home; the prodigal son who felt he could never deserve a home again was indeed welcomed by a loving father with an embrace and banquet of celebration. Though asking us to be pilgrims for a time, Jesus spoke of homecoming, warmth and greeting—of going to prepare a place for those who will no longer wander.

Loneliness, the opposite of being at home, one of the most terrifying of fears—that feeling of being forever unsettled and never at rest. Hospitality, at its finest, can help people become comfortable with themselves and, ultimately, should help to bring them home.

Hospitality can be offered in many forms—by an individual, a family, or a community in a large house of hospitality. But in order to be different from an institution, to be truly personal in offering hospitality we should have a sense of being at home with ourselves, in order to help bring someone else home—something possessed that can be shared. We should try to be people who can offer a gift and receive one, since often more is received than given.

Though Jesus was guest many times throughout his lifetime, his supremacy as host is brought out in his invitation: Come unto me, all ye that labor and are heavy laden, and I will give you rest.

Take my yoke (a yoke of forsaking all) upon you, and . . . ye shall find rest unto your souls (Matt. 11:29).

Luther Place Memorial Church is located where the richest of the rich meet the poorest of the poor. It is incredibly fertile soil for doing gospel.

A listing from the back of our Sunday bulletin spells out the range of our ministry: "Christ's hospitality is not just for us who formally worship together, but also—

> for the travelers who pass through this great central intersection of Thomas Circle in Washington, D.C.;
>
> for the dozens of neighborhood children who daily eat, learn, and grow in Luther Place Day Care Center;
>
> for the interfaith communities who live and work in Luther Place—*N Street Village*, helping to extend hospitality, satisfy hunger, clothe the wretched, heal the sick, comfort the imprisoned and distressed. These work in:
> Deborah's Place and Thrift Shop
> Zacchaeus House and Medical Clinic
> Barabbas Pre-trial House
> Bread for the City Center (emergency food and clothing)
> Bonhoeffer House
> Isaiah Refuge House (for teenagers seeking an alternative to prostitution)
> D.C. Hotline
> Cornerstone House (residence for full-time volunteers)
> for groups of youth and adults who visit and stay in Luther Place's Weekend Hospice;
> for people of the city who enjoy evenings of relaxation in the Luther Place Iguana Coffee House;
> for interreligious task forces on behalf of human rights of Soviet Jewry, people of South Africa, migrant workers, the disabled . . . ;
> for neighborhood and city groups, such as ProJECt (Protestant, Jewish, Catholic) community organization."

These represent continuing ministries of the congregation, but Luther Place also responds to special needs.

In the spring of 1977 we provided housing and office space for three weeks to a group of handicapped persons coming by plane from California to press the Secretary of the Department of Health, Education, and Welfare to end the delay in issuing regulations and the enforcement of existing legislation to assure accessibility of the handicapped to public places. (This unexpected visit awakened us to the inaccessibility of our century-old structure for physically handicapped persons. Within 24 hours we provided temporary ramps to the main floor, and replaced restroom partitions with handrails.)

In the frigid winters of early 1977-78 the ground-level social hall and the first-floor conference room and corridor space were opened as overnight shelter for the homeless men and women, respectively. Mats, blankets, an evening snack, and a hot breakfast also were made available. Up to one hundred persons a night were served.

For a week in the spring of 1978 housing was provided a group of persons who came to Washington to participate in a campaign against unjust torture occurring in countries around the world. The organizing communities, the Sojourners and Liberty to Captives, used the church facilities as "home base" from which to mount lobbying campaigns, liturgical demonstrations, and caucuses.

On any given evening three or more congregational or community groups ranging from a neighborhood choir to a group enjoying a vegetarian meal together may be meeting at the church. While in part supported by Luther Place funds and housing, few of the projects mentioned involve the full lives of Luther Place members, but the percentage of members involved directly or part-time in some one or more projects is increasing.

Financially supporting a church that has so many social ministry activities may pacify the consciences of some. Few would think of hosting the poor in their nicely furnished home dining space. But the very awareness of such personal contradictions demands attention that leads to growth and more fully integrated and gospel-oriented lives.

Slowly the connection between what happens at Luther Place on Sunday mornings and what takes place around and in the church on weekdays is welding together.

Frequently one gets the impression that unless one involves himself in hospitality in the communities of the Luther Place Village around the church, one is not being hospitable. Again it must be stressed that hospitality is an attitude, a way of life, and can be expressed in whatever place one works and lives.

4.
Walnut Street Baptist Church
Louisville, Kentucky
Robert A. Young, Associate Pastor

Bob Young is from Chattanooga, Tennessee. He has been at his present position since 1956. He earned the Bachelor of Arts degree at Carson-Newman College, Jefferson City, Tennessee, and received the Bachelor of Divinity, Master of Religious Education, and Doctor of Ministry degrees from the Southern Baptist Theological Seminary, Louisville, Kentucky. Young is an active member of the National Association of Church Business Administrators.

The Walnut Street Baptist Church is really the "First Baptist Church" of Louisville. It had its beginnings in 1815 when organized as the First Baptist Church in the small new settlement. Shortly thereafter a mission, the Second Baptist Church, was formed.

A few years later both First and Second were without pastors and both were in contact with the same man who would soon be graduated from Georgetown College. Both wanted to call him as pastor, and he led the churches to merge and to build a new meeting place. They acquired the property at the corner of Fourth and Walnut Streets in what is now the very heart of the downtown business district.

In the next forty-five years, the congregation grew to the point where it became evident they must have more property and enlarge their facilities. Property around them not being available, they decided to move to the corner of Third and St. Catherine Streets and in 1902 occupied the present facility. They moved to what then was one of the best residential sections of Louisville but since then, of course, has become central city. The church has occupied this property since the turn of the century.

Through the years Walnut Street Baptist Church has been prominent in the life of the city. We have a unique ministry not only because we are located in the center of the city, but about twenty thousand people still live near the church. Their homes vary from small inner-city apartments to very nice high-rise apartments, and about eight hundred government-subsidized new apartments for senior adults.

The growth of the church since 1900 falls into a pattern which really is defined by the pastoral leaders. Dr. Finley F. Gibson became the tenth pastor of the church in 1919, and at that time the total membership was 1,104 with an average Sunday School attendance of 450. He was pastor until 1941.

In 1942 Dr. Kyle Yates became pastor. At that time the average Sunday School attendance was 1,086.

Dr. W. R. Pettigrew became pastor in 1946 and over the next ten years significant growth occurred. In 1956 the average Sunday School attendance reached a high of 1,454. In the next two or three years, as was true with most central city churches, Walnut Street experienced a steady decline. Very concerned, the leaders took steps to evaluate where we had been, where we were, and where we needed to go.

During the late 1950s serious efforts were made to look at the community around the church and to evaluate the ministry, programs, and outreach of the church in relation to the community and the total metropolitan area.

A planning and survey committee was appointed to bring recommendations about ministries and outreach. The first committee that was appointed came to an impasse and resigned. Another committee was appointed and they likewise, after much study, determined that they could not put together recommendations for the future.

A third committee was appointed. A man with much experience in industry and planning for big business was chairman. The committee decided to involve the people in planning the church's future.

All three of these committees first faced the possibility of the church physically moving out of the city. All came to the conclusion that the mission of the church was to stay in central city—to minister to the large number of people still living around the church, and to provide a strong witness for the entire metropolitan area. The third committee brainstormed with every church group that had a meeting, asking them to dream about the next fifteen to twenty years in the life of the church. The committee asked, "What do you feel our church needs to do in the next fifteen or twenty years to stay alive and vibrant and to meet the needs of people both in the city and in the larger metropolitan area?" They emphasized that there were no limits—"feel free to suggest everything that you think our church could and needs to be doing."

From these brainstorming sessions more than two thousand ideas were presented by every Sunday School class, ladies and men's groups, Church Training groups, committees, choirs, and deacons.

The committee eliminated duplications and also put to one side those things that by the fondest imagination were just impossible.

One of the teenagers suggested we purchase the rest of the block which contained one of the largest hospitals in the city and the committee felt this was not possible. To show how the Lord works, about three years ago we purchased the hospital and the remainder of the block.

From all of these suggestions, the committee designed a survey which listed thirty-five matters from the brainstorming sessions. Four possible answers were indicated: yes, no, to some extent, or don't know.

Opinion Survey

1. Is the total membership of the church included in the planning, evaluating, and projecting of church plans?

2. Is there enough emphasis on real study and learning in classes and departments?

3. Should there be counseling service and aid for families in trouble?

4. Would you be willing to participate in visitation to the institutions of care in our church community?

5. Is a week-day kindergarten needed at our church?

6. Should adults in the Sunday School and Training Union be graded throughout according to relatively small age groups—after thorough information, incentive, and space is provided?

9. Do the Woman's Missionary Union and Brotherhood receive church-wide recognition—equal with the Sunday School and Training Union?

10. Would a change in the meeting time of Woman's Missionary Union Circle meetings make it possible for more women to participate?

11. Is the music ministry here a strong attraction to present and prospective members?

12. Should the opportunities for participation provided in the ministry of music be better known?

13. Is more practical training needed in personal soul-winning?

14. Are our worship services warm, vital, and satisfying?

15. Should our Sunday worship services be more informal in nature?

16. Is a larger seating capacity needed in the church auditorium?

17. Are two Sunday morning worship services the best solution for crowded conditions?

18. Should additional property be purchased for offstreet parking if other buildings are built?

19. Should all additional land available in the church's block be obtained as soon as possible for future expansion?

20. Is there a need for supervised weekday activities in our church for all ages in our church family and community?

21. Is the unified budget (this means only one church treasurer, not class, circle or organization treasurer) satisfactorily supported by all?

22. Are there too many "special offerings"?

23. Could money for future expansion be provided better through the sale of interest bearing bonds than through an outright loan from a financial institution?

24. Would it be better for our church to start one strong mission at a time rather than several weaker ones?

25. Should enrolment and attendance goals be adopted and attractively publicized for the next five years?

26. Is a much stronger program of advertisement and public relations needed to keep our church before Louisville's people?

27. Should nonresident, inactive church members be removed from our published church enrolment?

28. Are the following additions particularly needed on the full-time church staff in the immediate future?

    a. Minister of recreation

    b. Church receptionist

    c. Kindergarten director

    d. Associate pastor of counseling and visitation

    e. Primary and junior workers

    f. Music secretary—children's choir director

    g. None

29. Is more adequate up-to-date office space needed?

30. Would church staff efficiency be significantly improved by adjacent offices?

31. Are the salaries of the secretarial staff adequate for the present?

32. Are the duties of staff members clearly understood by the average active church member?

33. Should a strong planning committee be appointed to make and report building proposals to the church?

34. Is the need sufficiently urgent and our love of Christ sufficiently strong to justify commitment to this advance now?

35. If such advance is needed and in the will of God, are we ready to make the commitment?

I am a: Church elected Sunday School officer or teacher
_____ Church elected Training Union worker _____
WMU Officer _____ Brotherhood officer _____ Deacon
_____.

The results from the 732 surveys returned indicated some overwhelming consensus that gave direction to a report from the planning and survey committee.

Basically, the committee report said that the purpose of the church is to introduce men and women, boys and girls to Jesus Christ as Savior and Lord. The way to do this is through the many ministries of the church as contacts are made, relationships are established, and people become confident that the church really cares about them.

It was determined that our church needs to be involved in five areas: preaching and pastoral ministries, education, music, recreation, and social ministries. The report also recommended that in every one of these areas a full-time, top-level staff member be called in addition to the pastor. Some of the ministries were new (such as recreation) and would require new facilities. Some (such as education) would require additional or remodeled facilities. Some would require changing space, such as the social work ministry.

Since the report was made in 1960, practically every major move the church has made has been made in fulfilling the recommendations of this planning and survey committee, having been approved by the church.

When the recommendation was brought to the church, it was enthusiastically received because it was not a report from a committee stating "this is what we feel needs to be done," but it was a report from a committee stating "we have asked the members what they feel needs to be done and the report is what they indicated they felt God wanted our church to do."

The programs were developed to meet the needs of the neighborhood people and for the entire metropolitan area. For instance, the social work program meets physical, emotional, social, and spiritual needs of people around the church. However, people who live in the suburbs, who have expertise, want to come to our church to be involved in meeting such needs. This is our philosophy: we must minister to and reach for Christ the people who live in the city, but also the people in the greater metropolitan area, so that we can match the resources of the suburbs against the terrific needs of the city.

Very little was done except planning before Wayne Dehoney came as pastor in 1967, but with his dynamic and aggressive leadership and with many plans already made, the church has moved forward with tremendous strides.

The statistics on the next page tell the progress.

From the recommendations of the planning committee have come some philosophies which have guided the church through these years.

• See a need and meet it. On many occasions this has determined what has taken place as needs have been presented and as challenges have been made.

• The Neighborhood Development Corporation, originated by our church and the nearby Methodist church. Today it is a strong, thriving organization drawing many groups together to reclaim "old Louisville."

• Use mass media. The total church is convinced that television and other mass media catch the imagination of the entire city, an

1967—1977

	BAPTISMS	OTHER ADDITIONS	TOTAL ADDITIONS	BUILDING FUND	BUDGET	TOTAL RECEIPTS	AVERAGE SUNDAY SCHOOL ATT.
1967	80	143	223	$- - - -	$ 360,000	$366,897	1220
1968	77	177	254	- - - -	400,000	505,200	1132
1969	111	166	277	114,000	450,000	480,000	1067
1970	149	413	562	133,000	473,360	580,000	1042
1971	110	289	399	136,816	570,000	685,919	1111
1972	110	270	380	127,152	667,000	747,585	1203
1973	159	344	503	95,859	700,000	741,572	1330
1974	85	194	279	94,312	725,000	826,533	1464
1975	67	267	334	72,525	791,000	814,203	1358
1976	102	290	392	126,636	835,000	913,595	1454
1977	74	264	338	137,249	750,000	1,142,142	1436

```
            STATISTICAL RECORD 1967-77
             Walnut Street Baptist Church
                 Louisville, Kentucky
ADDITIONS
Total to Church....................... 3941
Total for Baptisms.................... 1124
Total by Letter, etc.................. 2817
Church Membership 1967 = 4761  1977 = 6245
Sunday School Enrollment
                  1967 = 1990  1977 = 3046
CONTRIBUTIONS
Building Fund .................. $1,037,549
Grand Total All Contributions... $7,803,645
```

absolute must in the central city church. About 70 percent of the people who have joined in the past eleven years have been first related to our church through the televising of our Sunday morning worship hour.

Our commitment throughout these past eleven years has been built around the knowledge that everything we do must be of absolute top quality. We must have the best in the entire metropolitan area! The best preaching, the best music, the best Bible teaching and study opportunites, the best community missions and social services ministry, the best weekday recreation, as well as the day-to-day operation and administration of church business. This will draw people to the church as their place of worship, work, and ministry.

One of the basic philosophies of our church through the years, even back in the early 1900s, has been that all people are welcome. Our congregation is a cosmopolitan group of people from many walks of life, many educational and cultural backgrounds, races and ethnic groups. We believe this to be truly a New Testament church.

The gospel is for everyone and in the fellowship of a church everyone ought to be received with compassion and everyone received alike. It does present quite a challenge when you realize that, for instance, on Sunday morning the worship service and all that is involved in it and the sermon has to meet the needs of PhDs, seminary professors, college, university, and seminary students, business people, politicians, doctors, and medical personnel, inner city people, adults who are functional illiterates, and others.

This is the challenge of the central city church. It is our contention that a church must come to grips with this and accept all people before it can grow numerically and in ministry.

The style of worship sets the tone of the spirit and enthusiasm of the church. Because of televising our morning worship service, we have constantly evaluated and redesigned our worship service. Each time we have made our service better for television, we have enhanced the service itself for the attending congregation. A conscious effort is made to provide music of all kinds, from Bach to gospel, and to have much congregation participation. It is a free, fast moving, enthusiastic, warm worship that meets the people where they are.

In central city there is a constant need for evaluating ministries and pinpointing groups which need a special ministry. This would be such persons as the deaf, the blind, single adults, and senior adults.

Our church saw the need to provide Christian-oriented housing for senior adults. A group of our lay members formed a nonprofit corporation and have provided a seventeen-story apartment building for senior adults. This is a government subsidized program and is separate from the church. This has been very successful and a large number of the people in the building are members of our church.

We have a strong single adult ministry, having designated a building for them. We have five departments through fifty-five years of age. We have a mailing list of about fifteen hundred single adults for different programs.

Another example is the ministry to the deaf with a Sunday School class and the worship service signed for them.

Our church provides two large houses for special ministry to young drug addicts or prison parolees. These are called "All The Way Houses." A wonderful lady, affectionately called "Earth Mother," has gathered money for remodeling and for operating the houses. Young people are assigned from the courts, or come to her directly, for help and they find a strong Christian program with Bible study and worship each day. She succeeds primarily because she presents Christ as the answer.

As we came through the study and planning process, we arrived at a very obvious conclusion that we had few adults between twenty-five and forty-five involved in our Sunday School. Within the past eleven years we have developed programs and Sunday School organizations especially for this group with a lot of our visitation aimed at the group. Now we have ten adult departments age forty-five and under.

We adopted the cafeteria programming philosophy. This means that just as anyone who tried to go through a cafeteria line and eat a little bit of everything presented would be sick, so one person cannot possibly be involved in every organization, program, and activity of the church.

We try to make programs meet needs of people, and then people relate to the programs which meet their specific needs. We do not try to involve everybody in every organization and every program of the church. We'd rather say to our staff and our committees and organizations that people become involved when you plan programs that meet their needs. If the participation in a certain organization is down, it is not the fault of those people who do not attend, but of those who do the planning.

The word *resources* has many meanings in the life of the church, but basically we understand it to mean leaders and money. In any central city church, much of the resources must come from the members who live in suburban areas. We must minister to central city and also to the entire metropolitan area to have the leaders and money to meet the needs of people in the city.

We emphasize personal stewardship with a budget commitment emphasis each year that challenges our people to become a vital part of the life of our church. Our budget has grown from $360,000 in 1967 to $1,000,000 for 1979. Also in that same time, our people have given approximately $1,200,000 over and above the budget for building and capital improvements.

A competent staff and the relationship of the staff to the lay members of the church is very important to a central city church. Our philosophy allows professional staff members to function to their maximum ability and necessitates relating in a very effective way to lay members.

Professional staff members have responsibility to relate in three areas. First, through committees and organizations, they plan with the lay members in their specific area. The success of all our programs depends upon the involvement of as many lay people as possible.

Second, the professional staff member helps enlist leaders. The important word here is "help," which doesn't mean that the staff member does all the enlisting. This applies in every area—for instance, all of our age-group choirs are directed by volunteers. A recreation and activities volunteer director is in charge every time the building is open, along with many other workers in each area. Of course, the educational program uses many volunteers as teachers, department directors, and officers. The social ministries area is constantly enlisting people to work in specific areas to meet the needs of others.

Third, the professional staff members train the volunteer leaders and multiply their expertise by training others how to minister. Training opportunities are provided, and specific help comes from the professional to the volunteer.

What does the future hold for a central city church such as Walnut Street? The entire area around the church is being redeveloped through the Neighborhood Development Corporation and other groups. Several professionals have bought older homes and are restoring them; one of our staff members has bought a home in the area and is restoring it.

Through our music ministry, we are beginning to branch out into community-oriented services. Last Easter our choir presented "Passion of Christ" at the Memorial Auditorium, drawing people from all over the city. At Thanksgiving the year before at the McCauley Theatre, the music ministry provided "The Freedom Festival" for the city of Louisville.

One of the most exciting things happening is the development of the hospital property on the other end of our block. Plans are being made to develop a full retirement center with approximately two hundred fifty apartments, and nursing home for middle and upper income people. This would give us an apartment house for senior adults on each end of our complex, and would certainly be a step in the right direction toward seeing the need and meeting it.

The future looks bright! We are at a point where tremendous growth can be enjoyed in the next few years with some added facilities and through the Spirit of God working in our people.

5.
Highland Avenue Baptist Church
New York City, New York
James S. Wright, Pastor

Jim Wright was born at Oliver Springs, Tennessee. He graduated from Car-son-Newman College and engaged in additional study at the University of Tennessee. He received his Bachelor of Divinity degree from Midwestern Baptist Theological Seminary, Kansas City, Missouri. Wright has served in various capacities as a Southern Baptist minister in New York since 1962.

This description of Highland Avenue Baptist Church in New York includes three segments. First, I want to relate what I found when I was called to the church in 1965. Secondly, I will discuss what has developed since that time, and thirdly, I will seek to explain where we are headed.

Only in recent years have Southern Baptists been planting churches in New York. Highland Avenue, founded in 1963 with forty-three charter members was one of the first. For most of the early days of the church, survival was a struggle. The size of the congregation was small as people would come but soon leave. When I arrived on the scene, I discovered sixteen remaining members of the church trying to serve a community of two million people, composed mainly of Jewish and Roman Catholic families.

To suggest that those sixteen members were discouraged is an understatement. No matter how hard they worked at it, the church kept on declining. Most of the earlier members were transplants from the south where Southern Baptists abound in great numbers, and they were accustomed to large, growing churches. However, what had proved successful back home simply would not work in New York City. The typical Southern Baptist approach to church organization and ministry led only to frustration and a feeling of defeat.

I found also that the church was in financial trouble. The prevailing thought at the outset had been, "If you want to start a church, do it like we always did at home—build a building and new people will come to join in a hurry!" A $92,000 sanctuary had been purchased but by 1965 the monthly mortgage payments, including interest, were not being met.

Another characteristic of the church which was most apparent when I arrived was the diversity of the members. There was a second generation Japanese couple from Hawaii in the group along with a couple from a rural section of Georgia. There was, in addition, an exiled Cuban physician and his wife, and a Brooklyn couple who had gone on job assignment to the Bahamas only to be converted by Southern Baptist missionaries. These people had very little in common except a deep and very real love for Jesus Christ and a persistent desire to present an evangelical witness to the area. That was the one spark of hope I saw in the face of overwhelming odds. They very seriously wanted a pastor to help them reach people for the kingdom of their Lord.

Aside from the problems mentioned previously, one of the first concerns we had was the way the church existed in isolation from the surrounding community. The sixteen members lived all over the city and would walk into the sanctuary for worship and then leave immediately. They did not know the people who lived next door to our building or across the street, and the local residents knew very little about Highland Avenue Baptist Church. We realized that one of our first tasks was to find ways to erase that barrier in the heart of Queens.

Since those days, we believe that God has led us to learn how to better penetrate an urban society with the message of Jesus Christ. We now have some thirty-eight nationalities of men, women, and children in our congregation with a total membership of over eight hundred. As new people have come, we have expanded our facilities and we are paying our debts.

During the worship services some seven languages have been used by translators (very similar to the way translating is done at the United Nations) to communicate the gospel being proclaimed. The Sunday School curriculum is taught each week in the four main languages of the area—Spanish, English, French, and Portuguese. Our church is one big family of different kinds of people fused into a Christian fellowship. We have had as many as eight hundred for morning worship and five-hundred for Sunday School, and it is clearly obvious to all of us that God is just beginning with us!

In retrospect there are perhaps twelve principles which have guided our steps in breaking down barriers and taking advantage of opportunities for ministry. Let me share them as follows.

First, we tried from the beginning to let our diversity work for us instead of against us. For example, the Hawaiian-Americans in the church knew other Hawaiian-Americans in the city; the family from Cuba were acquainted with other Cuban exiles in the area; and the Brooklyn couple knew many people scattered across the metro community. They were all encouraged to contact their friends and share the vision of our church with them. Soon new faces started showing up in our congregation, and this method of outreach has continued to be the main approach of our enlistment activities.

Second, we realized that we would have in the church only those persons we sought aggressively. As minority families moved into the area, we knew they would not join with us unless we first went to them.

Third, we were led to believe that God would send us talented, gifted individuals to assist in the development of the church, and God has done that time after time. For instance, the day came when we needed someone to translate our services into Japanese, but no one was available. Just then a man who had been a pilot in the Japanese air force visited our services, and I asked him to be our translator. Even though Ralph was not a Christian, he agreed. Several weeks later I called and made an appointment to see him because I wanted to talk with him about salvation in Christ. When I arrived, he indicated that he hoped I did not want him to stop being our Japanese translator! One Sunday morning six months later during a worship service, Ralph suddenly took off his headset and walked down the aisle of our sanctuary to claim Christ as personal Lord and Savior. Since then he has helped us reach numerous Japanese families. Our faith is stronger than ever that God will provide leaders for us as our work develops.

Fourth, we have not been afraid to venture into the unknown, nor do we try to control everything that happens. There are many people in our membership with whom I cannot speak except to say "good morning" or "how are you today?" or some other simple phrase I have learned in their language. The remainder of what I say to them is through a translator. Most of the time, I have no idea what they are talking about to each other, but I can tell they are enjoying their fellowship and maturing in their faith.

Fifth, we have been aware all along of the value of small Sunday School groups in the development of a diversified congregation. A number of people prefer to meet with others of their own race, and the Sunday School is a natural setting for such opportunities, especially for a church in a racially changing community.

Sixth, we have attempted to stay in close touch with the changes occurring in our community. I recently heard Ezra Earl Jones say at a National Conference for Churches in Racially Changing Communities that it is necessary for the pastor to spend half of every day, if at all possible, walking through the area around the church. I believe he is correct. A lot of our ideas for ministry have come from those walks through the parks and from sidewalk conversations. From such a journey came the origination of our nursery school which enrolled as many as two hundred children each week.

Seven, we have sought to stay open to the will of God as revealed through the hurts and experiences of our people. For example, we thought for a long time that we could not start a day-care center, because of space, time, personnel, and money. Then one morning at 4:00 I received an urgent call from one of our families who had come to us from Brazil. Both parents worked and they had been placing their four-year-old daughter in a neighborhood woman's home. Without the parents knowing it, the woman had been giving the children tranquilizers before she set them in front of the T.V. set all day long. The woman had overdosed our members' daughter and the child had died during the night. We started a day-care center the next day. I called one of our mothers from Colombia who had nine children and asked her to take charge of a day-care center in a basement of one of our homes. Soon the city found out about us and blew up because we were not meeting their standards. Eight years later we still are not fully approved, but we care for one hundred twenty children each day.

Eight, we try to remain open to the concerns of our own members. One week I realized that one of the most popular families in our church, a black couple, was no longer in attendance. I went to see them and learned that they were going to another church so their daughter could be enrolled in parochial school. The father, who was a city detective, and the mother, a nurse, declared that the public school system was too dangerous for their child. Soon our church decided to start a kindergarten which has since expanded through the fourth grade. We are making plans to include all twelve grades as we are able to do so.

On another occasion a young fellow in our congregation whom I had baptized came to see me. I was glad to see him and welcomed him into my office. After a few moments he looked me straight in the eye and said, "Pastor, I love and respect you, but you're doing things wrong in terms of your preaching." I almost fell over, but he continued, "You spend 95 percent of your sermon telling us how to receive faith in Christ and five percent helping us to know how to grow in the faith we have." He said it several times in different ways so I wouldn't miss the point. It shocked me, but I got the point! From this experience and many others similar to it, I have come to realize how much I need to listen to the members of the church. Now on a regular basis I sit down with individual members and ask them pointed questions about our work and how it can be improved. From young and old alike, I have received a great deal of insight.

Ninth, we have attempted to involve all our members, especially new Christians, in the work of the church. Many people in an urban church are unfamiliar with traditional procedures and organizational matters, and feel uncomfortable as deacons, Sunday School teachers, or finance committee members. Realizing this we have recently formed a dozen new committees which are being well received by our people. The committees are:

1. Bible Reading in the Home—the committee telephones church members about daily Bible study, and if the member agrees, some guidance material is mailed to the person.

2. Home Fellowship Prayer Meetings—the committee makes regular visits to homes for times of intercessory prayer.

3. Inactive Church Membership—Contacts are made with members of the church who have become lax in their attendance.

4. New Members—personal guidance is given by this committee to new members in such matters as Christian growth and church polity.

5. Missions—Visits are made to mission stations in the area to lend assistance as needed.

6. Sunday School Enlargement—Efforts are made to encourage persons of all ages to join our Sunday School classes.

7. Music and Youth—Support is given by this committee to the use of music with young people.

8. Elementary School and Day-Care—Contacts are made with the parents of our children to enlist the adults in the activities of the church.

9. Tithers for the Lord—This committee does not raise specific monies for the church but seeks through prayers and words of encouragement to create a mature spirit of tithing and giving throughout our fellowship.

10. Door-to-Door Evangelism—Visits are made each week to apartment buildings to talk with the residents about faith in Christ.

11. Subway and Open Air Evangelism—Once a week this committee goes into the subway and stands on street corners to discuss with individuals salvation through God's Son.

12. Summer Camp Enlistment—Contacts are made throughout the year with the families of our summer camp program to enlist the parents and other brothers and sisters in the activities of our church.

Tenth, real effort has been devoted to the systematic evaluation of existing programs. If something is no longer useful, we improve it, or discard it, or find a substitute. Vacation Bible School is an example. We came to the conclusion that we were not making much progress with the traditional VBS approach, so we converted it to a ten week summer day-camp experience. This is hard work, but one of the best activities available for the city child. Last year we enrolled more than five hundred children in day camp and the parents contributed over $50,000 toward our expenses.

Eleventh, we have been made aware that there are good days and bad days in the life of an urban church, and both extremes can happen fast, even on a daily basis. We have learned the meaning of sticking it out, no matter what comes our way.

Twelfth, in many ways we have come to realize that we cannot rest on the strength and success of the past year, or month, or week. Change in our setting occurs too quickly. We must keep our vision alive, our ability to be flexible and responsive as possible, and our faith in God active all the time.

What about our future? Our basic plan is to keep on doing what we are doing but expand it as needs arise. We are looking forward to the day when we will have one thousand children in our elementary school. We are planning for facilities that will accommodate five thousand people in worship and Sunday School, and the property for this expansion is being purchased.

We expect to see more of our number respond to the call of Christ for full-time work as ministers and missionaries and join with others from our congregation now serving across the nation and in other countries.

The more we do, the more we find to do! We are not quitters and the future is before us with more hope and possibility than at any time in the past.

Allow me to add a personal note. Highland Avenue Baptist Church has developed because God has watched over us and granted us the grace to stay together as pastor and people. I have gone through some traumatic experiences in my own life during the years I have been here, but the congregation has stuck by me. There were days when it would have been better for the church if I had been dismissed as the pastor because I was not able to do good for anyone. Yet they loved me and did not desert me. On the other hand there have been times I have had to stick with the church against my best judgement.

This is the special ingredient which the urban church must possess. The ability to be consistent, loving and forgiving, along with the willingness to stay put, is absolutely necessary. Short-term pastors in a rapidly changing community are a stumbling block for the church. The need for continuity on the part of the pastor cannot be stressed too much.

II
Inner City Churches

6.
St. Stephen's Episcopal Church
Boston, Massachusetts
William D. Dwyer, Vicar

Fr. Bill Dwyer was born in New York City, but he was reared in Jersey City, New Jersey. He is a graduate of Princeton University, and General Theological Seminary in New York. He has extensive experience in interracial and intercultural ministries, especially with Hispanics. He has been the pastor of St. Stephen's since 1963. Fr. Dwyer and his wife, Utako, have three children.

Boston's South End occupies an area bounded on the North and West by Back Bay and Copley Square, and on the South by Lower Roxbury. To the East is "Southie" which is the stronghold of Irish Catholics. It is here that St. Stephen's makes its witness.

The South End was and still is a "port of entry" for people coming into Boston. After the Civil War when some of the Yankee Protestant community moved out of Beacon Hill, the South End became the racially and economically diverse area that it is today.

St. Stephen's stood on Florence Street in the 1890s, but moved to its present site in 1927 on the corner of Pembroke Street and Shawmut Avenue at what is more or less the geographical center of the South End.

The neighborhood itself was designated in the 1950s as an Urban Renewal Area. This is important to remember, because much of the drama and tension of our neighborhood grew out of the struggle of contending forces over the form of "New South End."

Older and established neighborhood groups, dominated by landlords and homeowners, suggested a plan to the Boston Redevelopment Authority (BRA). Both lower income blacks and Puerto Rican residents were excluded from the urban planning process. The majority of black residents lived in substandard housing owned by absentee landlords. The traditional neighborhood associations did not demand adequate decent housing for these families. Public schools were poorly equipped to provide for children, particularly those from the minority community. It was not until the mid sixties that some improvements were made.

My own ministry at St. Stephen's began in September, 1963. My two predecessors, Fr. Bob Gardiner and Fr. Pastor Sotolongo, had worked to keep the church alive as a neighborhood parish.

Fr. Sotolongo was a young schoolteacher from Mantanzas, Cuba. During Sotolongo's time at St. Stephen's, Cuban refugees were coming into Boston in large numbers. Church agencies were lining up sponsors all over the country. The parish hall had become a center for Cuban refugee social activities and for an English-language program.

I had come from a seven-year ministry with the Lower East Side Mission of Trinity Parish in New York City. My own game plan was to continue to minister as faithfully as I could to the Cuban refugees in the parish, but also to attempt to regather a neighborhood congregation, some of whom had drifted away.

St. Stephen's had always been in the Catholic or "high church" Anglican tradition. I continued my predecessor's practice of having both an English and Spanish eucharist on Sunday mornings. I even resumed the practice of celebrating at 7:30 A.M. to meet the needs of some neighborhood people. Three services was a heavy burden for one celebrant, but frankly, I was afraid of losing the Cuban group and I was leery of a bilingual eucharist. So I continued to celebrate an 11:30 A.M. eucharist completely in Spanish (after a 9:30 A.M. eucharist for the English-speaking).

The two groups rarely got together except for a few sensitive folk on either side. The Cubans began to separate themselves and to seek other neighborhoods.

I had spent a number of hours trying to find jobs for Cuban businessmen and professional people. The language barrier kept them from entering the middle-class world of better paying jobs, status, and, respectability.

Not all the Cubans were "middle class." Hours were spent with one young man who had been crippled by polio. After years of emotional and financial dependency we found a job for him which lasted for several months. A great victory!

But the Cubans were leaving. Disillusionment with the church had begun. Although I was spending a lot of time visiting and trying to minister, I was an Anglo who spoke Spanish—and not a Cuban. But the pain of exile was intense, made more so by letters from home telling of hardships and of false hopes stirred by rumors of Fidel's imminent fall!

I cannot speak highly enough of the ministry of my wife to the Cubans, particularly several who lived with us. Our first child was not born until May, 1965, so that there was room in our house for people who in turn gave much to us.

With the Cuban "way stations" phase coming to an end, I had fewer and fewer people at the 11:30 A.M. service. In 1965 attendance had begun to fall off to the extent that I accepted the advice of a loyal Cuban communicant and combined the two later services into one. In late May of 1965 we had dropped the 11:30 A.M. service and moved to a predominantly English bilingual eucharist. Slowly a committed core of people began to emerge, including several of the Cuban refugees. Meanwhile a Puerto Rican community, made up largely of poor families, was developing in our neighborhood.

About this time, in the English speaking part of our congregation, a few people were ready for a ministry of outreach without too much regard for consideration of "church growth," and so was I.

Something should be said at this point about a remarkable succession of laywomen in ministry which has continued until this day. Helen Morton, a veteran of the National YWCA, has been in St. Stephen's for more than forty years. She has handled all kinds of thankless parish jobs and when she was well into her seventies, she began to study Spanish so she could take part in bilingual meetings. Whenever a 7:30 A.M. weekday eucharist is celebrated, she is in her place, a large, well-marked Bible by her side.

The women who have taken the job of church secretary have really been co-pastors. All have had a gift for listening. Margaret Norman who worked at St. Stephen's from 1963-1965 had a talent for writing. The newsletter which she put out helped us to build a network of supporting parishes in the suburbs.

Molly Ann Shera, a 1965 graduate of the Harvard Divinity School, started in the humble role of parish secretary. Without the status or fringe benefits that were built into my job, she created a role for herself as a lay minister and co-pastor working with young people, mostly black at first, and largely Puerto Rican later. With Marilyn Carrington, a brilliant and personable young black woman, Shera built up an after-school tutorial center.

The ministry of women added a much needed human dimension to the place. People felt free to drop in and talk. Often they were desperately lonely or depressed. I had always done a great deal of pastoral calling and felt free to do so because the parish hall was "manned" by Margaret, Molly, Anita Campbell, or other dedicated church members from the neighborhood.

The first response to a need in the community was made by a small group of St. Stephen's people working in collaboration with Dr. Mona Hull, an amazing and highly versatile lady who had founded an Episcopal day school in Boston. Hull came to talk to me about acquiring a small building in the neighborhood. Without the formal consent of our newly formed parish council, Hull and I put up out of our own money the purchase price of $3,300 for a small house at 379 Shawmut Avenue. So BEST (Boston Educational Service and Training) was born. It soon became apparent that to be effective, we would have to limit our function to testing and counseling children trapped in an unbelieveably inadequate public school system.

The Permanent Charities Fund, a prestigious Boston charity, recognized the value of what the tiny agency was trying to do to counteract the neglect of the school system. All kinds of benefits were held to raise money; yet Permanent Charities "cut us loose" (as is their policy) after three or four years.

Ultimately BEST was vulnerable because its Board was made up largely of black and white professional people. It was neither "grassroots" enough to satisfy the demands of the emerging black power and community movements, nor "establishment" enough to attract the money needed to meet the budget.

The time for "private entrepreneurship" of persons of goodwill was drawing to a close. Because the South End did not belong to one ethnic group but was multi-ethnic, the shock waves of "Black Power" did not hit for a while. But the stage was being set for confrontation between the BRA and a group which really did represent the submerged and neglected poor people of the neighborhood.

Sensing the inadequacy of the "one-to-one" approach to the problems faced by poor people, and riding with the tide of the Episcopal Church's newly awakened interest nationally in community organization, I had written a proposal for a Spanish-speaking community worker.

Church politics being what they were, the national church was eager to make a grant in Massachusetts since our diocese had always paid the largest (or next to the largest) quota!

Male chauvinists that we were, we believed that confrontation politics could best be done by a man! From the men and women who applied, a young Puerto Rican activist from New Jersey was picked. We formed a neighborhood advisory committee which included a social worker, the priest director of the Cardinal Cushing Center, and archdeacon Bob McCloskey, who helped plan the project.

Carmelo Iglesias, the young "action guy," was controversial. His ruling passion was the empowerment of Puerto Rican and black people who had been acted upon—rather than actors—in the whole urban renewal process. His style in public meetings was direct confrontation—table pounding, shouting and a series of dramatic exits. In these he was accompanied by a growing group of activists both black and Puerto Rican.

Until that point, the white liberals were the "approved" advocates of the powerless and they set the rules in the South End. One fact which Iglesia made us all face up to was the nonparticipation of the poor, especially Hispanics and blacks.

Iglesias started to build a small organization made up of Puerto Rican tenants. A rent strike was started on a street near the church and I was given the unofficial power of collecting agent for tenants.

A slum landlord was taken to court and found guilty for not giving heat to his tenants. His defense, of course, was that I was holding the money! Only three tenants out of twenty or thirty had held firm to the end and testified to the deplorable conditions in their buildings. The landlord appealed and a higher court found him not guilty.

The Episcopal City Mission managed to scrape together enough money for a second year of organizing, but there were now other "action people" in the field.

Iglesias had worked with Mel King, a highly respected black leader in the community. King was a director of South End House, one of the agencies of United South End Settlements. With the support of Iglesias and others, King made some financial commitments to a black-oriented Manpower Agency. His agency fired him and hundreds of people in the neighborhood reacted immediately.

This was the beginning of the populist movement which ultimately reshaped the policy of the Boston Redevelopment Authority. To heal the breach, United South End Settlements agreed to allow Mel King and other community leaders a limited time and funding to start a community organization. There was no agreement on goals of the new organization although a name, Community Assembly for a United South End (CAUSE) was chosen.

CAUSE began a "breakaway" organization magnetized by the strong leadership of King. Participation of whites was welcomed as long as they could accept black leadership and an abrasive style. The issue that the group identified as most crucial was housing.

The next three years were a time of greatly increased tension in my pastoral visitation. I was being drawn more and more into the orbit of the community activists. Between 1966-1969 it was the existence of St. Stephen's, as an established though small worshiping community with an openness to those around it, that made our involvement in social protest important at least as a symbol.

The long struggle of CAUSE involved demonstrations, taking over the building of the United South End Settlements and the local office of the BRA itself. The forced relocation of poor families and elderly folks out of the neighborhood became an issue as important as the failure to get new housing built.

The turbulent history of CAUSE reached a peak in April, 1968, with a series of protests ending in the weekend blocking off of a private BRA parking lot. Arrests were made including Mel King, Carmelo Iglesias, our parish council member, Bill Knight, and myself. The pictures in the Boston *Globe* of the incident made our group notorious in some quarters, but pleased others who believed in non-violent direct action.

CAUSE had made its point and with a new BRA director and a new mayor eager to build a new political base, the climate became favorable for emerging tenant-based organizations.

What has saved St. Stephen's time after time has been the unexpected appearance of the right people to meet a need!

Peter Lawrence, a young Harvard graduate and newspaper reporter, worked three years as a virtually unpaid volunteer setting up a tutoring program, working with youth, and acting as a family case worker.

Molly Shera recruited Stephen Moss, one of a number of young black leaders, as a co-worker in programs aimed at teenagers in the Cathedral project.

Shera had the gift of reaching out in love to teenagers. Some of the girls, particularly in the Puerto Rican community, came to the church for baptism, confirmation, and marriage because of her witness. The great struggle of the sixties was trying not to allow our Christian witness to be pushed completely into the background by an emerging nationalism. Our Christianity was too white and too afraid of real dialogue and conflict. On the other hand, a group of us believed that however much we might distort the message, we were called to be ministers of Christ.

Marilyn Carrington and Molly Shera hit upon a new means for raising money for our summer day camps (which we had run since 1964). They wrote letters to suburban churches asking for sponsors for each boy or girl in the day camp. In return for a $30 camp "scholarship," each sponsor received a handsome certificate with the name of the child and a progress report.

Shera was committed to the doctrine that to win a hearing for

the gospel, a person must earn the right to be heard. With the
rising tide of black power and self-determination, the attempt to
reach across racial barriers was extraordinarily difficult. It is to Shera's
credit that she communicated love across the barriers as well as
she did, and that St. Stephen's was perceived as being in some
ways a part of the struggle.

Times were particularly troubled in the late 1960s. In a class at
the Episcopal Divinity School (EDS) I was accused by a black seminarian of feeding my own ego by working in a black and Puerto
Rican neighborhood. Deeply hurt by this, I was ministered to by
a black priest, a Panamanian working in a midwest parish, whose
coming to St. Stephen's for a Sunday was a gift of God's grace.
These experiences, as I reflected later, were the living out of what
we celebrated in the eucharist.

Around 1970, Huston Horn, a seminarian from EDS, found two
large timbers in the rubble of a demolished building. He lashed
the beams together, rusty nails and all, and with the blessing of
the parish council hoisted the huge cross up over our old stone
altar and hung it on by a steel hook on the sanctuary wall. It is
by no means a pretty sight, but it is the most arresting liturgical
symbol in the church building. As a comment on the situation
that many of our community face every day, it is powerful, a visible
Word of God.

At a time when heroin addiction reached the epidemic stage in
the South End, Shera started a drug education program. Assisted
by three young black men, this education program grew into an
established South End Drug Council. The leaders were young and
the style abrasive. As usual, there was fierce competition for the
few "crumbs" handed down by the establishment, as represented
by the government or the private foundations. There were rumors
of violence and of possible shootouts in the parish hall that failed
to materialize. But they kept us nervous!

The constructive result of all these was a drug education program
in the Boston Elementary schools that made youthful drug addiction
its main concern.

Perhaps most important to the development of the community

by members of St. Stephen's was the contribution of time and talent to two tenant groups (one black and one Hispanic) which were successful in renovating or building houses for people of low income. In general our men and women have been highly motivated and have gotten deeply involved in the life of the parish. The organizational ability of Dick Lampert was crucial to the initial success of ETC (Emergency Tenants Council). This organization, now independent, is called IBA (Inquilinos Boricuas on Accion). Through many house-to-house meetings, confrontations with landlords, and bargaining sessions, a junkyard was removed from the area, housing was leased from the Housing Authority for sixteen Hispanic tenant families, two hundred units were built for the elderly, and over two hundred family and single units were completed.

We have learned that the people of the old community are the backbone of the new community. They lived there all the while and they were not turned into urban nomads.

Valuable assistance for us came also from Charles and Mary Glenn. Charles is head of the Bureau of Equal Opportunity in Massachusetts and has served as a vital liason between the diocessan planners and our church. Don Williamson, an HEW executive, priest and lawyer, led our church school and worked with us in planning. His wife, Annie, also assisted in many ways. John Russell, a retired priest (who died in 1978), dedicated his time mainly to the visiting of elderly people in the community.

One effect of our efforts, and particularly of the Christian witness of Helen Morton, a seventy-year-old community activist, was the coming of Dona Paula Oyola and her family and of Natividad Cotto. These formed the basis of a Spanish-speaking group to replace the last Cubans. I started to run house Bible studies in Spanish and occasionally celebrated a house eucharist. Soon we established a 7:30 P.M. Wednesday evening Spanish service which has served as an alternative to the Sunday bilingual eucharist.

In the 1970s we entered into a somewhat less turbulent era.

A committee appointed by the parish council in 1970 attempted a reorganization of the church's ministry. The four areas of ministry identified in 1970-1971 were worship and music, housekeeping, education and witness, and neighborhood outreach. More recently they have been expanded to sixteen sub-ministries in four major areas: worship, growth in Christ, building the church, and witness and service.

The majority of active people at St. Stephen's have been strong advocates of poor people. We are heterogeneous, but white middle-class people who are attracted to our church are drawn to us because of our openness to the community.

As we envisioned the areas of ministry in 1970, each was to be carried out by a task force of lay or clerical ministers. The convenor of each task force was accountable to the vicar (me) and the council.

The total budget (minus summer program) in 1964 was about $20,000. Now the budget is more than $90,000 with aid from the diocese. Largely thanks to the efforts of a couple who belonged to our church for only one year, Robert and Barbara Melville (Bob as canvass chairman, and Barbara as parish clerk), our pledging rose from about $11,000 in 1976 to $16,000 in 1977. The other money comes from grants from Episcopal City Mission, a local "Walk for Hunger" group and suburban churches with whom we have built up a relation.

For the past four years, Alberta Detrés has been doing the secre-tarial job as well as a large part of the youth ministry. She is the heart and soul of our ministry to people. She has known much pain and tragedy in her own life and she is willing to listen to others, including the broken and battered who sit and wait for their Social Security checks.

From 1970 until 1976 it seems that St. Stephen's was the one church in Boston which was both multiracial and self-consciously an "urban parish."

But we are a struggling church. Our Sunday School, despite the dedicated labors of some gifted people, has been an area of real difficulty. We are ministering to many children in an urban culture whose parents don't come to church. A platoon system of teachers was tried last year but it lacked continuity. This year we have teachers whose commitment is more solid.

Ironically as the sense of mission to the city is revived, the relatively few resources available will be further taxed. Worker-priests may become the norm, and some of us who have been full-time clergy may need some career redevelopment.

St. Stephen's is a small part of the total Christian ministry to a highly complex, varied, multiracial community. We have shared ministry with other groups such as the nearby Roman Catholic Cathedral, Holy Cross; the Emmanuel Gospel Center; and the Salvation Army Harbour Light Center.

When a Spanish Pentecostal Church burned in 1974, we allowed the congregation use of our church for evening services. We have not tried to be a "bridge church" as Episcopalians like to think of themselves, but we have tried to respond to the needs around us.

After much struggle, a food cooperative was started. Following a year of running it independently, the decision was made to join a larger food cooperative (Mission Hill). It remains predominantly middle class in spite of strenuous efforts to include poor people, especially Spanish-speaking people.

A ministry to people in need off the street has always been carried on in some way or other, mostly by the clergy. Beginning in 1975 John Douglas, a former journalist, and social activist, assumed the role of minister to transients. On the theory that this ministry is one carried on in the name of the whole diocese, funding was secured from Episcopal City Mission in April, 1977. Hundreds of men and women have gotten at least an initial interview and referral. We try to distribute assistance so as not to develop dependency.

Karl C. Williamson, a talented young seminary graduate, has made a five-year commitment to starting a youth ministry. He, like some others at St. Stephen's, has been radicalized by his urban experience. He is backed by an advisory group of people who care about our teenagers.

Our church more or less reflects the composition of the neighborhood which is 30 percent black, 30 percent Hispanic and 40 percent white. We have some eighty families in our parish plus at least seventy single persons.

The sustaining power of liturgical worship is something that ought to be stressed in churches like ours. Somehow we are constantly reminded that our *story* is included in God's *story* of redemption and grace. The continuity of prayer and worship in the liturgy gives identity. The "point" of liturgical worship combines with the "counterpoint" of being flexible and ready to change our ministries to meet changing conditions.

One achievement we are very proud of is the compilation of a bilingual Holy Eucharist-Rite II service book with a handsome cover designed by a local artist. The work was done by four Spanish-speaking Anglo members and one Hispanic (Cuban) man.

Our three buildings (the church, vicarage, and the parish hall) have been in bad condition for years. In 1976 we applied for a $22,000 loan from a special diocesan fund called the Stokes Fund. Eventually our request was approved. We hired Michael Pierce, a layman, to be a full-time maintenance supervisor. Two fires set by an arsonist (unknown) in the winter of 1978 (after the blizzard) nearly destroyed our parish hall. Thank God for the church insurance company!

Since 1977 we have been trying to do a better job of establishing specific goals and objectives as we proceed with our witness. We are particularly concerned about strengthening our evangelistic ministry. A bilingual committee has been formed and is visiting in teams of two, starting with nonactive members.

Many more things could be said. Above all I want to express my profound gratitude for the hundreds of Christian men and women, rich and poor, black, Hispanic, and American white, who through their prayers and giving and working have helped our church remain viable over the years. Our growth has not been remarkable but slow and steady. People have left us whose loss seemed irreplaceable at the time, but the Lord has given us new people to carry on.

7.
Grandview Baptist Church
El Paso, Texas
William G. Perdue, Pastor

Bill Perdue completed his undergraduate work at Baylor University and earned the Master of Divinity degree at Southwestern Baptist Theological Seminary, Fort Worth, Texas. He has been the pastor of several churches, all in Texas. He is married and is the father of five children. His hobbies are jogging, golf, and softball.

El Paso, Texas, is a city unique in its location—because it shares a common border with Old Mexico and New Mexico. A current population of four hundred thousand makes El Paso the fourth largest city in Texas and the second fastest growing city.

Juarez, Mexico, El Paso's sister city across the Rio Grande, has 750-800,000 people and will reach one million by 1980. Because of its proximity to Juarez, El Paso is the second largest crossing point in the United States for undocumented aliens. Last year, nearly one million illegal entrants were apprehended and deported by the Immigration and Naturalization Service. Some of the reasons for the mass influx are stark economic figures: half of Mexico's eighteen-million-member labor force is unemployed; a devalued *peso* has sent prices spiraling; the country's 3.5 percent population growth is one of the world's highest. Border Patrolman Michael S. Williams commented, "They're starving to death down there."

In addition to three cultures represented in El Paso: Indian, Spanish, and Anglo, there are twenty thousand military troops and their dependents stationed at nearby Fort Bliss and White Sands Missile Range. The city's senior citizens are among the fastest growing segments of the population. El Paso is one of the greatest mission fields in the world.

In the midst of such a vast mission opportunity is our church, Grandview Baptist Church, a member of the Southern Baptist Convention. The church, organized in 1927, was then in an all-white neighborhood in one of the better sections of the city. By 1950 the community was 80 percent Anglo and 20 percent Spanish speaking. Today, it is 72 percent Mexican-American and three percent black. Schools in the neighborhood are 95 percent Mexican-American. It is estimated that one day the community will be 100 percent Spanish because of the rapid Mexican-American increases.

Property has been devalued, and the area has been in a state of decline for the past twenty years. City planners for the central area predict that unless trends can be reversed, the future is rather bleak. Younger families with children will continue to move away, and the older people will find it increasingly difficult to maintain their homes. Then, the little neighborhood shops, schools, and churches will begin leaving the area. The planners report that a way must be developed to stabilize home ownership and restore the desirability of housing.

Grandview Baptist has always had a strong mission emphasis. Prior to 1960, our church established five other churches in the greater El Paso area: Loma Terrace Baptist Church, Skyline Baptist Church, Rosedale Baptist Church, Kemp Street Baptist Church, and Morningside Baptist Church. In 1960, we averaged 612 in Sunday School, but during 1963 the Chamizal Treaty with Mexico relocated thousands of Mexican-Americans in the Grandview addition. As Spanish-speaking persons began to move in, Anglos moved out, and the church steadily declined. By 1975, our Sunday School attendance had dropped to three hundred. Our building had deteriorated along with the neighborhood, and rapid pastoral and staff changes brought feelings of uncertainty and discouragement.

I came as pastor of the church in April 1974. It was my feeling immediately that we needed to elect a long-range planning committee to study the needs of the church. The following question was uppermost in the minds of the committee: should the church relocate or should we remain and attempt to reach the Mexican-Americans in the community? The church made a unanimous commitment to remain in the neighborhood and develop ministries to reach our section of the city.

The long-range planning committee report contained six major recommendations:

1. That the church build completely new facilities for our Spanish Mission located only six blocks from our church. Financing will be arranged with the Church Loan Corporation of the Baptist General Convention of Texas, Grandview Baptist Church to pay one-half of the monthly payments on the loan and the Spanish Mission to pay one-half. Further, a five-year Program of Advance be implemented at the Spanish Mission to lead the congregation to become an independent church by 1980. Salary reduction to be made annually for a period of five years to lead the Mission to become self-supporting.

The Spanish Mission was at that time worshiping in a twenty-by-twenty foot building which was an eyesore to the community. There were no Sunday School classrooms, no parking, and nothing that would appeal to the largely Spanish neighborhood. With the help of a church builder from the Texas Baptist Church Extension Department, Grandview Church immediately erected one of the most beautiful facilities in El Paso. Today the Mission averages one hundred forty in Sunday School and is rapidly becoming the largest Baptist Spanish work in the city. Grandview continues to pay one-half of the building payment and part of the Mission pastor's salary.

2. That the Building Committee proceed with plans for the construction of a Family Life Center Activities Building with a desired goal of beginning work on it in April 1975. The Center was to have a gymnasium and recreational facilities to serve the people in the church and neighborhood.

Construction on the Center began exactly one year after my arrival as pastor and was completed in October 1975. The ten-thousand-foot building ministers to the needs of a multi-racial neighborhood.

3. That the church secure the help of the Stewardship Department to lead in a Together We Build Program with a goal of retiring the indebtedness in three years. Because of the extreme transiency of our membership, this was later changed to five years, and we are on schedule.

what of a Spanish Church.

4. That the Church secure an Activities Director for the Family Life Center to develop and implement plans for reaching Spanish-speaking persons.

5. That the church develop an active military outreach to the thousands of personnel stationed at nearby Fort Bliss.

As a result of this outreach, army doctors and nurses who joined Grandview began a desperately needed medical ministry in the little village of El Faro, Mexico, sixty-five miles down the river. Through the assistance of the Baptist General Convention of Texas, the El Paso Baptist Association, and several upstate churches, a church has been started, a parsonage has been built, a full-time pastor has come on the field, and a beautiful medical clinic has been erected for the people of El Faro and in nearby villages.

6. That the church launch a program of stewardship training to develop a greater mission outreach to our state, our nation, and our world.

A second long-range planning committee was elected in 1977 and came with two major recommendations:

1. That the church purchase property in northwest El Paso and establish a satellite congregation to meet in the school building adjacent to the property. In eighteen months the satellite will revert to mission status and a pastor will be secured.

At the same time the Grandview area was deteriorating, the northeast area of El Paso was exploding in population. When it became evident that no other church in the city would begin a new work there, we purchased property near the proposed freeway. Again with the help of the Church Loan Corporation Department of the Baptist General Convention of Texas, Grandview began a satellite ministry in the school house. Both the pastor and staff worked for sixteen months. In the spring of 1978 the satellite became a mission and called a young seminary graduate. The Apollo Heights Baptist Mission is showing rapid growth and will begin erecting a building in the next few months.

2. That we begin a Spanish Department in Grandview with adult Bible classes only. Youth and children will be integrated in our Sunday School and a pastor will be secured to lead a Spanish worship

service simultaneously with the main English worship of the church.

Because the Spanish mission services were in Spanish and many Mexican-American children speak English, a Spanish Department was begun in Grandview in the fall of 1977. The Department is now averaging forty people per Sunday, and it has a pastor who serves on the Grandview Baptist Church staff. The children of the department attend the Grandview Sunday School and worship with their parents in the Spanish language.

Presently, declines have leveled off in our church. The Sunday School averaged 487 in 1978, and total gifts have risen to $243,000. The Spanish department has a weekly average attendance of forty, the Spanish Mission has an average attendance of 140, and the satellite congregation averages seventy weekly.

Our church is multiracial. In addition to our Anglo families, we have three black families, seven Spanish families, two families from India, one Lebanese family, one Puerto Rican family and one Chinese family. Teaching English as a second language is part of our Sunday School curriculum. We also have a weekly jail ministry, a strong cassette homebound ministry, and active women's and men's organizations.

Our Family Life Center is used at nights by both members of Grandview and its missions. The American Association of Retired Persons meets in the Family Life Center, and the present task force is seeking to develop a senior citizen day-care program as well as a nutrition program for the elderly in the community. The building is open on Saturdays for neighborhood children in a guided recreation program. We believe, however, the center is underutilized and we are seeking an Activities Director.

As a result of all of these ministries, a new mission consciousness is growing among the people of the church. Throughout my pastorate here, the main focus of my work has been to lead the members to have a concern for the people around our church. I have tried to provide a theological and biblical base for all that has been accomplished. Phil Sims, deacon and chairman of the church's medical committee says, "Our pastor is a strong Bible preacher and teacher who lays a solid biblical foundation for our varied ministries. The people have caught his optimistic outlook and are willing to follow his leadership. He never ceases to commend the people for every accomplishment."

Mrs. Leon Magers, long-time church member and Woman's Missionary Union leader said, "The pastor is the key to a mission-minded church. Unless he gives the people a vision and challenge, the work is severely hindered. Our pastor gives full support to the Baptist Women's and Baptist Men's organizations, and he preaches missions all the time. He has been the key to our strong mission outreach."

Tensions have arisen at almost every recommendation; they were caused not so much by racial attitudes, because the church is racially mixed, but by economics. The changing community and the moving of families to better sections of the city caused an erosion of the church's financial capabilities. In particular, there was major opposition to purchasing the property in northeast El Paso to begin a satellite congregation. Rumors that the pastor was trying to relocate the church were soon dispelled and the work progressed in a remarkable way. As tensions grew and opposition developed to the expanding ministries, I wrote out my resignation several times. I just never did turn it in. But the people had and have a mind to work, and God continues to bless us.

Whatever we have accomplished could not have been done without the help of the El Paso Baptist Association, the Baptist General Convention of Texas, and the Home Mission Board of the Southern Baptist Convention. We received $5,000 from the Care and Share Fund of the Texas Convention, salary supplements for our mission pastors, excellent leadership from our mission extension department in Dallas, especially Dr. J. V. Thomas and Vaughn Manning, and invaluable help from Bruce Bowles and the Church Loan Corporation. As I look back over the years of a ministry in a changing community, I am amazed at the assets we have in our Southern Baptist Convention leadership.

8.
Allen Temple Baptist Church
Oakland, California
J. Alfred Smith, Pastor

The Reverend Dr. J. Alfred Smith was born in Kansas City, Missouri. He earned the Bachelor of Science degree at Western Baptist College, Kansas City, and the Bachelor of Divinity and Master of Theology degrees at the Missouri School of Religion, University of Missouri. He received a second Master of Theology degree at the American Baptist Seminary of the West and was awarded the Doctor of Ministry degree by Golden Gate Baptist Theological Seminary, Mill Valley, California. He is the author of seven books and has written numerous articles for religious publications. He has been at Allen Temple since 1970.

The area occupied by the cities of Oakland, Alameda, Berkeley, Piedmont, Albany, and part of San Leandro was originally inhabited by scattered tribes of Coastonian Indians. The approximate same area was granted by the Mexican Government to Don Luis Maria Peralta who came to California with the Army expedition in 1775. Peralta divided the land among his four sons, giving the area primarily encompassing what is known now to be Oakland to his third son, Vicente Peralta. He developed it into an important shipping point for tallow, hides, and for the exporting of redwood logs.

In the 1840s squatters came and a small settlement began to grow. With the onset of the gold rush, enterprising Americans from the East came, bought portions of the land, established an important shipping point to supply the resultant mining activities inland, and eventually incorporated Oakland (named for its many oak trees).

The central Broadway district developed by 1860 and the population grew to 1,543. As a center for rail transportation for Northern California, Oakland's population spurted to 10,500 persons by 1870. Another decade brought cable cars and with the federal government's dredging of the channel, Oakland became a deep water port, bolstering the city's economy. The central business intensified and expanded so that by 1890, 48,682 people lived there.

The 1906 earthquake did some damage, but Oakland escaped the massive fire which ravaged San Francisco and sent many homeless victims on to Oakland. In 1936, completion of the San Francisco-Oakland Bay Bridge ended Oakland's isolation from San Francisco.

World War II created many wartime jobs, drawing people into Oakland and many other Bay Area communities, and provided its current population base.

The city of Oakland began to decline after World War II. The rate of decrease in the number of residents from 1950-1970 has diminished each decade. However, the decrease during those years was only 6 percent which seems to be insignificant. What is significant and not apparent are the changes in the ethnic and age composition of the population involved, the related changes in overall income, and purchasing power.

Oakland's white population has declined since 1945, both in absolute numbers and in relation to other ethnic groups. By 1970, the white portion of the city stood at 59 percent compared to 95.2 percent in 1940. Both black and white numbers increased following World War II, but the black and other nonwhite percentage gain each decade far exceeded that of the white until 1970. Thirty-four of every one hundred were black and forty-one of every one hundred were of a nonwhite minority.

The declining white population is attributable to the exodus of whites to the suburbs from the city. Gains in the population were made essentially by the black minority. Between 1950 and 1960 the growth was 36,000 and between 1960 and 1970 41,000. The total black population of that ten-year span rose by 77,148 or 162 percent, while the number of whites decreased by 35 percent.

The population characteristics of the city's blacks are substantially different from those of the city's whites. Whites are generally older, have higher incomes, and have fewer children. Twenty of every one hundred whites are sixty-five or older while six of every one hundred blacks are sixty-five or older.

While the movement of a number of Oakland's whites has been

from the city to surrounding suburbs, the primary movement of
Oakland's blacks has been within the city. This movement and
the resultant distribution of the black population within Oakland
has been influenced by Federal, state, and locally developed programs.

A large portion of the population is poor, young or old, and
unemployed. Oakland has one of the highest unemployment rates
in the nation and members of ethnic minorities form a disproportion-
ately large segment of the city's population. Consequently, the city's
poverty rate is extremely high. Sixty-four percent of Oakland's poverty level residents have either black or Spanish surnames. Yet the
combined two groups comprise only 45 percent of the total population. Fewer than one in eleven white Oakland residents are at poverty
level, compared to one in five Spanish-speaking and one in four
black residents.

What all these changes in the population structure mean for
the future of Oakland is that even if white out-migration and black
in-migration were somehow brought to a halt, black population numbers would continue to make gains on the white and predominate
by virtue of the females (other things being equal). And too, if
population trends continue as they have in the past, the new majority
will be of low income with an increase in the number of those
that are now at or below poverty level. Oakland will also have an
increase in both the old and the young, the least economically productive segments of the population. The low purchasing power of
these groups combined will no doubt have a tremendous effect on
the central district's desirability as a business location, its function
and its configuration.

In the year 1919, on the corner of East Fourteenth Street and
Seminary Avenue, in the eastern portion of the city of Oakland,
J. L. Allen organized a Northern Baptist black congregation in a
little half-like building. At that time the dominant population was
comprised of Portuguese and middle-income nonblack people.
Masses of Afro-Americans lived in West Oakland because of the
railroads, and service-oriented jobs were situated in that part of
the city.

Seven years later, after J. D. Wilson and R. H. Thomas had served sacrificially as mission pastors under the Northern Baptist Convention, the membership changed the name from Eighty-fifth Avenue Baptist Church to the Allen Temple Baptist Church.

Under the leadership of Pastor G. W. Wildy the task of enlarging the facilities became necessary and ground breaking services were held October 29, 1939. Through hard work and sacrifice the building of a little chapel on Eighty-fifth Avenue and A Street was accomplished.

While the Rev. Dr. C. C. Bailey served as Pastor of Allen Temple, major expansion of the facilities was accomplished. On July 17, 1960 a ground breaking service took place. A new sanctuary which was to seat 550 people and educational facilities were added.

In recent years, the mortgage was paid, the Thomas Center was erected, several lots were purchased around the church, and parking facilities were added. A beautiful parsonage was purchased in 1971.

At the present new, spacious facilities are being added to meet the needs of a growing congregation. In the meantime our two worship services on Sunday mornings are packed to the walls with people of diverse backgrounds. Our commonality comes at the point of knowing Jesus Christ as Savior and Lord.

Allen Temple has come a long way. In 1919 the membership was twenty-one. Today there are more than 2,300 members with over nine hundred families in the congregation. The median age is thirty-seven, and we have a full program of Christian education, music, and community ministries staffed by outstanding aggressive lay leaders. The church now holds affiliation with both the American Baptist Convention U.S.A., and the Progressive National Baptist Convention.

The community surrounding Allen Temple, predominantly white at one time, is now 90 percent black. The various racial components are reflected in the church membership: black, American Indian, Chinese, Mexican American, and white. The majority of the members are black. The greatest growth of Allen Temple has occurred over the past twelve years as definite efforts have been made to reach and be of service to everyone regardless of age, race, social condition, or culture.

We have received numerous awards and citations from many groups, due mainly to our ministries in the community. Some of the awards have come from the N.A.A.C.P. Chapter of Oakland; the American Baptist Churches U.S.A.; The Black Panther Party; the City of Oakland; the Boys Clubs of America; the California Legislature; the Spanish Speaking Unity Council; and the Oakland Filipino-American Association. Recently the New Oakland Committee, composed of the business, labor, and minority leaders of the city, established an annual J. Alfred Smith award for the community leader who has done outstanding work at the grassroots level.

The ministry of Allen Temple is the work of the members and not just the pastor and church staff. Each January all elected officers of the church are required to spend four Sunday evenings in training sessions for leadership and service. Then every effort is made to give the laity all the freedom needed to carry out their responsibilities and be leaders in the fullest sense of the word. I give primary leadership to the training classes. The main text we study is William M. Pinson's *The Local Church in Ministry.*

This past year our church officers and leaders held a retreat at Clear Lake, California, for the purpose of evaluating all existing programs and activities. The retreat theme was "Building for the Future Together." Some eighteen pastors and urban church leaders from across the nation were there to assist us in making tough decisions about our work, and in devising plans for the future expansion of our witness.

When the Black Panther Party moved its national headquarters to within a few doors of our building, we immediately met with them to determine areas of disagreement and of mutual concern. From hours of heated dialogue came a common goal to help build the city of Oakland into a more humane place to live and work. We entered into such projects as:

• Providing at Allen Temple a ministry to prisoners and their families;

• Promoting cleaning up the neighborhood by sweeping sidewalks in the ghetto business area, and encouraging merchants to act more responsibly in improving the city;

• Gathering a coalition of community groups against racism within

the Oakland Police Department;
• Opening Allen Temple to become the center for voter registration programs.

Over the space of several years a number of Black Panthers have become Christians and joined our church.

The church program includes housing and real estate seminars, dental clinics, and medical checkups. We believe the church in society should be prophetic but also priestly. We have gone many times as pastor, deacons, and Committee on Christian Social Concerns to meet with the Oakland City Council and the Alameda County Board of Supervisors to discuss the causes of the poor and the powerless in our city. We have engaged in hearings with the County Welfare Department and the Juvenile Justice officers about case workers who demonstrated little compassion for clients and decisions of judges which reflected injustices. We have tried to be an advocate for the sake of righteousness and fairness.

Our members are proud of the fact that Allen Temple is used often as a teaching model of urban ministry by two Bay Area educational centers, namely, Golden Gate Baptist Theological Seminary, and the American Baptist Seminary of the West. We are looked on as an example for practice in ministry and for understanding the relationship of the local church to its community.

John F. Kennedy once said, "In the life of every nation, as in the life of every man, there comes a time when a nation stands at the crossroads; when it can either shrink from the future and retire into its shell, or can move ahead—asserting its will and its faith in an uncertain sea."

Allen Temple Baptist Church might well be at the crossroads. We can become proud and arrogant about our beautiful facilities and ease towards becoming a club for the comfortable, or we can move even more to being a powerful voice for the kingdom of God where righteousness flows as a mighty stream. We are planning for the latter.

9.
First United Presbyterian Church of Allegheny
Pittsburgh, Pennsylvania
David A. Neely, Pastor

The Reverend David A. Neely is the son of Presbyterian missionary parents who served for many years in Cameroon, West Africa. He came to America at the age of twelve to go to school and received his advanced training at the College of Wooster, Wooster, Ohio, and at Princeton Theological Seminary. In 1948 Neely and his wife, were appointed as missionaries to Metet, Cameroon, by the Board of Foreign Missions of the Presbyterian Church, U.S.A. From 1953 to 1972 he served as a professor at Dager Theological Seminary in West Africa.

The story of First United Presbyterian Church of Allegheny begins almost 150 years ago. People in the area of the North Side of Pittsburgh, Pennsylvania who have known First United Presbyterian Church of Allegheny recall that in the past it was a church of the elite. With its Scotch-Irish tradition, the church had pastors of strong academic training. The formal worship had little appeal to the down and outer.

During its heyday, in the 1920s, the church supported a number of missionaries in Egypt, Ethiopia, and Pakistan. In fact, First Church at one time was considered to be the most prestigious church of the North Side, with a membership of around sixteen hundred at its peak—in 1931 there were 1,324 on the roll—many of whom were well-heeled professional people. At one time the richest people of the city lived on the North Side. I am constantly reminded of these facts by some of my parishioners who remember the good old days and hope and pray that the church will be filled with good, upstanding, prosperous people, as it used to be.

The church was organized on October 27, 1831. Services were held in a building called "Semple's Long Room" on the west side of Diamond Street, Pittsburgh. In less than five years, the congrega-

in the inner city, ministry respect, is not a matter of education but effeciercy!

tion had outgrown its accomodations and the building was enlarged to seat one thousand persons. Later, in 1867, the church purchased its present site at 815 Union Avenue.

There was a decline in church membership, prestige, and influence in the 1930s when many of the successful affluent members headed for the suburbs. Some diehards, however, were stubborn enough to keep their roots where they were.

I came to First United Presbyterian upon returning to the United States from my post in West Africa. I knew working in this parish would be tough for the church had been without a pastor almost two years. It wasn't a plus that many Presbyterian clergy would be interested in. But without boasting, I am certain my years on the rugged frontiers of the mission field prepared me for the challenge.

I moved from one jungle to another. I believe there are as many non-Christians per square foot on the North Side of Pittsburgh as there are in darkest Africa. I came to Pittsburgh and began my ministry there on January 1, 1973.

North of the church the racial complexion is diverse. 46.5 percent of the population was black in 1970; today it is higher. In this area, 728 arrests were made for major crimes in 1972, more than twice the rate for city-wide Pittsburgh.

Many parishioners hesitate to leave their homes at night for fear of being mugged. A number of our senior citizens who attend church at night have been assaulted. Some have had a car tire slashed, or had a battery or car stolen.

West of the church emerge high-rise apartments and a shopping mall. Only 3 percent of the population in this neighborhood received public assistance in 1972. Most of the 306 arrests in the neighborhood in 1972 involved larceny. The area still is occupied largely by whites, yet more and more blacks are moving in.

To the south, townhouses have been constructed recently. It is estimated that 95 percent of these houses are occupied by blacks with low to modest incomes.

To the east of First Church is "Dutch Town" named for residents of German descent who came over from the old country to work

in factories such as the nearby H. J. Heinz Company. Our membership is peppered with names such as Behringer, Ehrenberger, Hersh-
man, Schultz, etc. About 90 percent of the population in this area
is white. Almost a quarter of the neighborhood received public assistance in 1972 compared to 14 percent city-wide. Statistics confirm
the problem of poverty in this section.

The highest percentage of people are represented in the sixty-
five and over age bracket. On the East North Side 21.6 percent
of the people are sixty-five and over, whereas for the city as a whole,
it is 13.5 percent. About 20 percent are five to nineteen years old.

Next door to the church, is Martin Luther King, Jr. Elementary
School with 775 students, approximately 60 percent black and 40
percent white compared to a 60 percent white—40 percent black
ratio in 1973. The students are not bused, so the school is a community barometer. Its changing ratio indicates the transient nature
of the population: as many as sixty new students a month enroll
at the school. Two blocks away at Allegheny High School, the current
enrollment is approximately one thousand which is eighty-five down
from the previous year.

The median school year completed by those living on the North
Side is nine. About 30 percent are high school graduates.

To say the least, our church is surrounded by a changing population. There has been a decline in the number of people as many
move away. This mobility and transiency make it difficult for families
to take root in the community.

When I came to First United Presbyterian Church of Allegheny,
I was overwhelmed with the challenge: what could a small church
of about 170, mostly aging members, do to turn things around?
As I entered the sanctuary of my new assignment to preach, the
seats were half empty. I had a sinking feeling I was ministering
to a dying congregation.

I began to realize that I had to develop a new measure of success.
How successful would we have considered Jesus Christ to have been
at the conclusion of his earthly life? He chose twelve disciples,
not a mighty successful army of two thousand persons. Jesus seemed
more interested in quality commitment than great numbers.

After prayerful consideration and consultation, our members decided to have a planning retreat at a nearby camp-ground. Twenty-four members of our Session, Board of Trustees, and deacons, plus key members of the church went to Camp Crestfield October 19-20, 1973, to decide where we were and where we were going as a church.

We determined that the purpose of First Church was to minister and to witness to the people of the community, and thus, fulfill our responsibilities to Christ through service and love.

The group decided to concentrate on renewal, leadership development, stewardship, and racial integration. This looked impossible, yet, we knew that with Christ's help all things are possible.

We considered our assets: one was a one thousand-member Community House right next door. What had to be done was to break down the barriers that for many years had separated the church from the Community House, and to get members of the church involved in the mission arm of their own church.

We sought spiritual renewal, not through human manipulation, but through the Spirit of God. We experimented with prayer groups and Bible study and worship forms.

I had seen the joy of the resurrection of our Lord in African worship. They clapped, they danced, they participated in dialogue as the minister preached. I wanted the same spirit of worship for First Church.

We developed a song sheet including such songs as "They'll Know We Are Christians By Our Love." We sang and we even clapped! The worship service increasingly has become a glad celebration.

Recently, we changed the front of the sanctuary. A large platform with moveable furniture was constructed. We have had a liturgical dance, beautifully performed by a suburban church. Excellent choirs have joined with our own. Old hymnbooks were replaced with new ones.

Our order of worship has been transformed. I spend a lot of time reading Scripture and in prayer. Preaching is one of the most important parts of my ministry. I have tried different kinds of sermons. Several times I have led a twenty-minute inductive Bible

Study on a passage of Scripture; the congregation sometimes participates with questions. We tried dialogue sermons, and at the beginning of worship, we have a children's sermon.

Visiting the sick, the shut-ins, the lonely, and the bereaved is important. I believe such visitation demonstrates Christian concern. One reason for the higher than normal attendance of our members on a Sunday morning has been due to the visitation ministry. Not only do I make visits, but a committee of the Unicameral Board sends a card to the sick and the shut-in members each month. Also, one of our senior members devotes herself to a telephone ministry.

People who have known the church for many years have come back to worship with us in recent days. They have remarked that they notice a difference in our spirit. It is more friendly. It is more loving.

The Community House involves all ages, from toddlers to senior citizens.

After a careful survey of senior citizen needs, we launched a Saturday luncheon program. We had no idea how the senior citizens would respond. Sixty showed up at the first lunch, each making a fifty-cent contribution for the meal. Now the program has grown to more than a hundred. Response has been so enthusiastic that some persons come two hours before the meal. Volunteers serve the tables. An *esprit de corps* has grown among them as they discovered how much fun it is to wait on others. Many people linger after the meals to chat or to get involved in crafts or crocheting or to play games. Four senior citizen clubs meet weekly. They call themselves the "North Side Friendship." A number are new members in our church.

April 12, 1977, a group of concerned members of First United Presbyterian Church went to Fairfield, a Presbyterian camp, for a twenty-four-hour retreat. We sat down again in order to consider the future of our church. Many options were discussed. The most important decision that came from the retreat was to seek an assistant minister who would concentrate his efforts in the area of Christian education in the Community House.

Wayne Campbell Peck, Phi Beta Kappa graduate of Denison University in Ohio and Harvard Divinity School, turned down more lucrative offers to work in the Community House. Enthusiastically and imaginatively he has put his shoulders to the wheel, developing new programs, all geared to introducing people to the Christian faith.

He initiated an after-school Christian education club for the adjacent Martin Luther King, Jr. Elementary School. Forty children (60 percent black, 40 percent white) come twice a week for worship, learning about the Christian way of life, playing games, and working with crafts.

On two afternoons, students are offered supervised tutoring. The program is intended not only to improve the reading, writing, and arithmetic skills, but to bring to them the realization that the church cares.

One of my dreams for the First United Presbyterian Church of Allegheny is for it to become a true fellowship of reconciliation.

Elayne Johnson Hyman, a black theological student at Pittsburgh Seminary, came to our church to work as student minister in the Fall of 1975. Elayne had a Master's Degree in Russian literature from the University of Pittsburgh, plus a beautiful Christian personality. I wondered how a black woman would be accepted in our congregation, for I knew the prejudices of some of our people. I had heard one of our members say: "As soon as those coloreds start coming into our church, I'm leaving." And I had heard one of the black leaders of the city say that Pittsburgh was like a big plantation.

I brought Elayne to the personnel committee of the Session for an interview. She won the committee over with her sincerity and charm. Having crossed our first hurdle I wondered what kind of reception she would get from the Session itself. After a period of questions and answers we went around the group for a vote. Every elder but one voted affirmatively.

I wondered how the congregation would receive her. My objective was to break down gradually, one by one, racial prejudices and to change attitudes. Elayne won the hearts of the congregation little by little. She loved to visit, and she and I spent endless hours in homes with the sick and shut-in. She conducted and assisted with funerals.

Elayne has a gift for putting words together. Her sermons were well received, and our congregation was proud that upon graduation from Seminary she was the recipient of the homiletics prize. She expressed the desire to join our church. I wondered what kind of response there would be. There was no dissenting vote in Session when she asked for membership. Everybody welcomed her gladly. The day she left us as student minister, the one member of Session who had voted against her came up to embrace her. She had won his heart, too. There was hardly a dry eye in the congregation when she said, "Goodby." She loved the congregation, and they loved her.

Though we still have a long way to go, I believe our congregation has made some progress in changing attitudes. For example, in the Community House with approximately one thousand members, 40 percent of whom are black, we see in the After School Club black and white children and youth playing and learning together in a beautiful way. The fellowship of reconciliation I dream about is coming, but oh how slowly! The seeds have been and are being sown.

While our church may not be successful by standards of the world—in terms of multitudes of conversions and new members—we are not finished yet. The Spirit of God is working in our midst. He has made us more sensitive to one another's needs and to the needs of our community. If there has been any success in our congregation, ultimate credit goes to God who makes all things new. It is true that we are struggling, but by no means are we dead. We are very much alive!

I believe strong leadership in the church does not mean exploitation, manipulation, or domination; but serving and caring. The minister in the inner city takes his cue for leadership from him who took the towel and washed his disciples' feet.

10.
Liberty Park Baptist Church
Mobile, Alabama
Jack Maples, Pastor

Jack Maples is a native of Whistler, Alabama. He received his Bachelor of Arts degree from Mobile College and has done graduate work in institutional counseling at the University of South Alabama. He and his wife, Joyce, have two daughters. Maples has served twice as the pastor of Liberty Park.

Each Wednesday evening at our church, we hold a prayer service. Recently during one of those services I asked the group to write out their personal reflections about the church and help me with this case study. These comments resulted:

> Where Christ is, people are like a family. That is the way the church is now. I have been a member here for twenty-three years. During those years we have seen many different people come to us. I teach children in Sunday School. When one of them draws a picture, writes on it, 'I love you,' and puts it at the place I sit, what does it matter whether the child is black or white? They are God's children and I love them.—Susie Fisher

> When the community started to change, it meant a loss of members from our church. Those of us who remained wondered if we could survive. For one thing we had an enormous debt to overcome. Through hard work and prayer the debt was paid in full in two years. Some of our former members have tried to hinder us in our efforts to remain in this community. We have found it hard to understand them, but we have tried to forgive them through the help of the Holy Spirit. At first we thought in our despair that we would have to sell the church property and move, but then we remembered the covenant we made with God when we were organized. We had promised to be a candle lit for him in the neighborhood. That settled the question for us.

We decided to remain and keep our light burning for our Lord.—Kathleen Lavene

I am the wife of the pastor of Liberty Park. To say that I did not have prejudice would be untrue. Everyone has prejudice of one form or another. However, I was taught by my Christian mother and Sunday School teachers that God created man in his image and that it's not what a person looks like on the outside that's important but it's what he is on the inside that counts.

My husband has served twice as the pastor here. The first time he came, he had just finished college. The church was a small mission and he helped organize it in 1954 into a full church with adequate facilities. We met and were married during those years. Then we were led elsewhere to serve. About ten years ago the church called us back. Although the attendance was good when we returned, the church had gone through a financial crisis. Jack sat down with the leaders and explained to them how to set up a budget that would work. Within a short time the church was financially sound again.

When we returned we knew that the immediate neighborhood was about to change racially because it was happening not many blocks away. Also, the school system was under orders to desegregate and the parents were upset. My husband began to preach that all mankind is created by God and that we shouldn't support missions in other places if we were not willing to worship with all races of people at home.

Watching the church decline in numbers and finances has not been easy to accept. The one thing we have tried to instill in our children and our church members is that God never promised us that everything would be rosy. Instead, he promised that whatever we have to do or experience he will share it with us and help us see it through.

I feel that the pressures on us because of the changes in the community and in the church have drawn my husband and me closer to God and to each other. —Joyce Maples

I used to pass by Liberty Park Baptist Church and wonder about going there because it was so close to my home. I did not go in however because it was a white church and I am black.

My grandchildren started going to Vacation Bible School at the church and then Sunday School. They wanted me to go with them. The pastor stopped by many times and invited me to church. One Sunday I decided to go and my grandchildren took me to the adult ladies' class. I walked in late but they all greeted me with beautiful smiles and words. I went to the 11:00 A.M. worship service and Brother Jack introduced me to everyone. I started attending everything. A few weeks later the pastor talked with me about church membership, and after a lot of thinking and praying I decided to join on Mother's Day, 1977.

Our church is one of the best churches in the world. I might say, we truly love and care for everybody, whether in times of sickness or good health. We love by words and deeds.

This is just part of my feelings about the church. With time and a good mind, I could write a book about it!—Clara Belle Brooks

When we had a church full of people we did not do nearly as well as we do now with only a few. It has proven to me that God is behind us and wants us to keep on spreading his Word. We have become a much closer church family and a happier one. Our pastor likes to ride his bike all over the neighborhood seeking people. He has found so many who need our church for food, clothing, and Bible study. We give more to missions than we ever have and our worship services are more spiritual than I can ever remember. We really get close to God.—Delores McNeil

Christianity has always played an important part in our lives. Being black, there have been times when our faith has been put to the test. It has troubled us how two races could read the same Bible and yet practice a white Christianity and a black Christianity. It has been our prayer and hope that somehow this situation could be alleviated. As we understand the Bible, a church should open its doors to serve people with no regard to race, creed, color, or previous conditions. We became members of Liberty Park with apprehension because of past practices, but we believe in the church and what it stands for. It has been a great spiritual inspiration for us to be part of a church like this one. We are seeing Christianity at its finest hour and we are proud to be in the membership.—**Lena and Robert Weaver**

This church was built as a place of worship and service for our community. Many members left and we lost leaders. When crucial decisions came, we prayed harder and harder, and our fellowship increased. We have learned that all things can be accomplished through Jesus Christ. We plan to keep up our work for him.—**Clara Twilley**

As these statements indicate, Liberty Park Baptist Church is now a small, struggling inner-city congregation with a very big heart and a Macedonian pocketbook. The church building is on the corner of Cotton and Rice Streets in a section of Mobile called Crichton. An old saying about Crichton is, "Born and raised in Crichton and ain't scared of nothing but thunder and lightning." Some of the people are not even scared of that!

Our church is made up of a very warm and open group of people who are willing to give God every opportunity to work through them. But it was not always like this.

Going through social change has a sobering effect upon a church. They become closely knit and learn how to appreciate and take advantage of each new day as a chance to lift the name of Jesus Christ. In doing so they begin to find a sense of peace with God and are able to look with strength at the disappointments that beset them.

There are victories to be won, setbacks to endure, and dreams to be realized. These things can be done when the people learn to love others and are loved in return. They start to discover that it's never too late to learn how to grow and share. As our church decreased in size we grew in spirit and closeness.

The neighborhood around the church building changed almost overnight. A "for sale" sign went up in front of a house and within a few days the dwelling was bought by a black family. Whites began to move away in a mass exodus. The church was devastated. During 1973-74 we dropped from 175 in Sunday School to thirty. No matter what we tried, the steep decline continued. We thought we were ruined.

Before this time the church staff consisted of a pastor, a minister of music, a secretary, an organist, a pianist, and a custodian. Within months the pastor was the only one remaining.

We hit the bottom. There was nowhere to turn except to completely trust in God to understand our pain and lift us up so we could move forward.

We faced our alternatives as squarely as we could. Should we disband, sell the property, and give the proceeds to Southern Baptist Convention mission causes and college scholarships? Should we relocate? After weeks of prayer and discussion we decided to stay and open our doors to all races of people. That was our turning point even though it was hard for some members to accept. On a Sunday night we gathered for confession and commitment at the front of the sanctuary, and our journey began.

Today some of our folks refer to us as the "complete" church because of the racial and social diversity of our fellowship. We have made much progress. At the beginning we didn't have any hope of continuing to meet the mortgage payments on our property, so we started a paper collection drive. It caught on and within two years the debt was paid. We began to realize what we could attain and that God was not through with us yet.

We decided to live out of our weekly tithes and offerings and not go into debt for anything. We increased our percentage of gifts to missions. Before long our offerings became larger than at any time in the history of the church.

We decided to eliminate committees and bring every business matter before the congregation so we could all be part of the decision-making process. We decided to forget our plans to build a youth building and a new sanctuary, and put our resources into reaching and serving people.

After a survey of our community and surrounding areas, we found there was still a need for our church to serve both races. Many of the whites were older and lived on monthly Social Security checks. We began to contact the white and black residents to let them know we were remaining in the neighborhood and desired to be their friends. Slowly some individuals began to take us seriously.

We started to develop a family atmosphere where every person is important. We introduced flexibility into our worship services with more music and open dialogue at times between preacher and congregation. Major attention has been given to the study of basic biblical principles. We decided if something we are doing does not work, we will stop and find something that will. We have not had time to waste on unnecessary matters.

Our emphasis has been on evangelism and service to others. We have conducted many classes on personal witnessing and have trained workers in various phases of Christian social ministries. Our people have transported older residents to grocery stores; taken meals to shut-ins; gotten hospital equipment for homebound patients; started a dial-a-friend ministry; provided an apartment for families of out-of-town hospital patients; visited at local nursing homes; given money and food to needy families; and started a "Big A" Club for children after school.

Every decision is crucial, or so it often appears. We are always planning and developing something. Progress is slow but our gears are still in forward and the word "retreat" is no longer in our vocabulary.

Occasionally our sanctuary is full on Sunday mornings as we worship, and what a joy it is to observe the crowd. However, it is still depressing to see vacant rooms not being used for Sunday School and mission study.

Because of rapid changes in our work, my emotions fluctuate between rejoicing one day and deep sadness the next. The burden of meeting financial responsibilities is at times overwhelming. So many things which need to be done are ignored because the money is just not in the treasury, but we have learned to take what we have and do the best we can. My family could not make it if my wife did not work, and there are moments when my ego needs get to me when I remember that her wages double mine. Also, it really hurts when fellow clergymen at pastor's conferences talk about the small size of our church, label us as being a social gospel congregation, and seek to proselyte our members.

At the same time—and this is impossible to explain—I cannot thank God enough for giving me the position as pastor of Liberty Park Baptist Church. Our people are so loving and compassionate. They seem to sense when I am low and they reach out to give me a boost through their words, actions, and spoken prayers. They have become committed to Bible study, fellowship, and mutual prayer, and I love being their pastor.

God has truly been wonderful to Joyce and me. He prepared us slowly for each new step we have taken. To say I have not been scared at times would be false. I have been forced to realize that before I can lead the church to be Christ-like, I must first get my own prejudices in hand. When the first black person came to join the church my knees were trembling even though it was a wonderful event for all of us.

When members leave and the money drops, I get discouraged. Yet, as we make it through one tense situation after another, it seems to give me courage to face the next one. Preparing this case study has helped me see how much more our church could have done and how much needs to be done. It has been a humbling yet challenging experience.

III
Suburban Churches

11.
Vienna Baptist Church
Vienna, Virginia
Lawrence E. Matthews, Pastor

Larry Matthews' hometown is Norfolk, Virginia. He is a graduate of the University of Richmond and Southeastern Baptist Theological Seminary, Wake Forest, North Carolina. He has done advanced work in pastoral counseling and is now completing additional graduate work at Princeton Theological Seminary. Matthews and his wife, Jean, have four children.

The small town of Vienna in the northern Virginia suburbs of Washington, D.C., had more than doubled its population by 1955. It was in July 1955 that Vienna Baptist Church began as a mission of the First Baptist Church of Clarendon, an older suburb in Arlington County.

A number of young member families had moved from their Clarendon apartments to purchase the less expensive homes that were rapidly being built as a result of Vienna's proximity to the new beltway. With support from the sponsoring church and the state and local associations, the mission was able to have a resident pastor who led services in one of those new houses.

The mission soon was constituted as a church with 122 charter members. Again with financial support from sponsors, land was purchased and a building for worship and education was occupied in 1958. A full Southern Baptist program was implemented from the very first and the church experienced growth commensurate with the growth of the town and surrounding county. By 1965 members had increased to 571 with 909 names on the Sunday School roll.

When the organizing pastor resigned, a new pastor was called in 1961. Under his leadership the church became involved in the church renewal movement. Key leaders attended renewal conferences at Southern Baptist Theological Seminary in Louisville, Kentucky. As a result of contacts made at these conferences, dialogue began with Gordon Cosby and the Church of the Savior in Washington, D.C.

Some members felt the church should move toward a mission-centered, outward style of ministry in contrast to an institutionally-centered program aimed at numerical growth. Inevitable conflicts arose as the church began to struggle with its own self-identity. As one member later phrased it in a written history of the church, "For a growing number of members, the vision of a 'servant' church relevant to the realities of the late 20th century became a stimulus and a possibility."

When the pastor resigned in October 1965, the congregation acted upon a recommendation from the deacons that "a working group . . . make an exhaustive study relative to the church's program, policies, procedures, and/or any other matter of concern that may be elicited from the church membership and make specific recommendations to the church for adoption." The church had decided to move forward with an in-depth self-study.

The study group conducted surveys within the congregation; led self-studies by committees and organizations; evaluated the constitution, by-laws, and articles of faith; and recommended the election of a committee to call a pastor.

I look upon the process of my call to the church as a significant part of the task in which the congregation was engaged. Open and honest dialogue was characteristic of my contacts with the pastoral call committee; an evening of no-holds-barred dialogue was held with all deacons and their spouses. A similar question and answer evening with the entire congregation in the fellowship hall followed a Wednesday prayer service.

The varied points of view, fears, and hopes were discussed in an atmosphere that was amazingly open to personal differences and the leadership of the Holy Spirit. It was that quality of sensitivity that led me to accept the call of the church during the summer of 1966. Here was a suburban church willing to pay the price of self-awareness and self-giving that is necessary for effective ministry anywhere, especially in metropolis.

The dialogue between study group and congregation was intensified during my first year. Conflicts surfaced and were dealt with at retreats and meetings. More than once I was grateful for the training in group dynamics and group leadership I had received through the Church Training Department of the Baptist General Association of Virginia. The study group continued to lead the church's self-study while examining constitutions, organizational manuals, and other such documents of Baptist churches from all over the country. For almost a year I led the church in a study of Baptist history and thought on Sunday evenings.

The study group decided to write a manual that would simplify the church's organizational life. As each section was written, sessions were held with the congregation for suggestions. The new organizational structure was officially adopted by the church in June 1967. In addition to church officers and other committees, four main groups were established at the heart of the church's institutional life: a missions committee (to research needs for outreach ministries and guide the church in its mission action); a Christian education committee (to shape and staff the church's Christian education ministry); an administrative committee (to be responsible for budgeting, property management, etc.); and a diaconate (freed from administrative responsibilities, to assist in the pastoral care of the congregation and to lead the church's spiritual growth and development).

This organizational style was designed to be easily modified to meet the changing needs of both the congregation and the community. The manual has been amended frequently and remains a dynamic document. It contains an original covenant, an invitation to and definition of membership, a statement on the ordinances of baptism and the Lord's Supper, and a list of denominational and ecumenical affiliations.

In 1969 I was invited to be a member of a Home Mission Board study group on the suburban church. All members of our group studied and discussed the book, *New Congregations*, by Donald L. Metz. The author's thesis is that a congregation (especially a new one) faces a constant temptation to substitute institutional survival for its formally stated goals as a Christian people on mission. The more generalized the formal goals, the more easily such a substitution can be made.

Metz's book was the focus for our diaconate retreat that fall. The deacons decided to lead the church to clearly identify its goals in 1970. During the study, it became clear that our newly adopted covenant adequately expressed what our members understood to be the goals of our congregation. The diaconate then decided to move the covenant to a more central place in our church's life. A Book of Covenant was created and on Palm Sunday, 1971, after months of careful preparation and instruction, the congregation filed forward and in a graphic act of rededication signed the Book of Covenant.

Every month since then as we join in the Lord's Supper, new members come forward, sign the book and then read the covenant with the rest of the congregation as we commit ourselves to each other in the love of Christ. The covenant reads:

We believe that the Church of Jesus Christ is called to live under His Lordship and continue His ministry to the world. We therefore covenant together as a local expression of His Church to:

. . . engage regularly in the worship of God, Bible study and opportunities for growth in the Christian faith.

. . . live in Christian love and forgiveness in our families, congregation and relations with all people.

. . . fulfill our Christian vocation through the stewardship of life and possessions both within and beyond the congregation.

. . . proclaim the Gospel through words and deed to those whose lives ours touch and provide the resources necessary for others to do so throughout the world.

But changed structures do not guarantee effective ministry. It became the responsibility of the missions committee to survey community needs; members were challenged to respond to these. When one of the Woman's Missionary Society circles decided to become a mission action group, the church had found a model for practical involvement in mission. This first group focused upon the needs of senior citizens in Vienna and, ten years later, this mission action group—composed now of both men and women—leads a monthly fellowship and maintains an ongoing person-to-person ministry with more than 155 senior citizens. The WMU concept was thereby adapted to our particular needs and similar mission action groups were formed around literacy, a ministry in Appalachia, and the issue of low cost housing in Vienna. The group concerned with low cost housing invited members of black and white congregations to join in an effort to stimulate such construction. Although no housing resulted from the effort, we learned to run the risk of failure and we established communication with the sizeable middle class black community of Vienna. Later when Washington, D.C., erupted in civil disorder as a result of Martin Luther King, Jr.'s death, the communication proved valuable.

Immediately after the civil disturbances, the church asked outside resource people to lead in special studies. The guest leader for one of these sessions, the pastor of a black D.C. church, pointedly asked if the church really wanted to get involved in the needs of the city? Convinced that such was the case, he suggested that we look for an inner city congregation that had a specific ministry with which we might become involved.

The Israel Baptist Church, a black congregation in northeast Washington, was sponsoring a weekday youth center ministry in a row house owned by the church. Since the church needed additional money and personnel, representatives from the two congregations met and joint sponsoring of the ministry began in the fall of 1968.

A mission action group was formed around this concern and, based upon the trial year's involvement, one half of the center's budget was included in the 1960 Vienna church budget. A board of directors, composed of pastors and members of both congregations, began a cooperative ministry that deeply affected the lives of not only many youth of northeast Washington, but also the members of both congregations.

Vienna members have led programs at the center. Children from the center have participated in field trips to the Vienna church house and have attended our summer church camps. The two congregations have exchanged pastors and choirs and shared in special youth Sunday services. The board of directors meets regularly in each other's church and homes.

Board members have faced and worked through racial stereotypes and fears, and honest disagreements.

Members of both churches have had to learn how the other church does things, and each has been instrumental in challenging or inspiring the other at crucial times. I am convinced that a shared commitment to a common ministry has made possible not only an effective witness to inner-city children, but Christian growth for members of both churches.

The church's openness to ministry was also challenged in 1967 when the Cooperative School for Handicapped Children requested the weekday use of our educational building. Those severely handicapped children and their dedicated teachers were a constant inspiration until the school became a part of the Fairfax County school system in 1973 and moved to its own building.

In 1971, we started devoting one Sunday morning worship service in early fall and spring to mission action: presenting needs and making commitments to specific ministries. Mission action groups are then formed around those concerns. The missions committee appoints coordinators and monitors the progress of each group. New church members are confronted with mission action needs as part of their orientation.

As needs are met or commitment to a specific ministry ceases, that particular mission action group is discontinued.

In 1977, about 175 members were involved in mission action. Groups have been formed around sponsoring a Vietnamese refugee family, outreach visitation, nursing home visitation, neighborhood youth ministry, clothes closet, new member orientation, world hunger, and foster homes for teens.

Also, the missions committee has led the church to participate in other denominational and ecumenical ministries. Vienna Baptist Church is a member of Community Ministry (C.M.), an ecumenical effort of thirty churches from most of the denominations in Fairfax County. C.M. employs a community minister who focuses and coordinates the resources of the churches to effect change in the secular institutions which determine to a great extent our quality of life. Concerns have included the elderly, juvenile justice, drug problems, housing needs, poverty, and health care.

The church also helped found and participates in CHO (Committee to Help Others) which was organized by lay volunteers from most Vienna churches to provide emergency assistance to persons in dire need. A direct relationship is maintained with a couple under appointment by the Foreign Mission Board of the Southern Baptist Convention. The missions committee faces the continuing challenge of calling forth volunteers for all of these ministries as well as constantly confronting the congregation with other needs.

Worship was the church goal most mentioned in the 1970 congregational study. Since 1970, members have been invited to join the staff in planning worship services. These worship planning groups study principles of Christian worship with special emphasis upon the free church and Baptist traditions. Not only has this practice resulted in an enlarging group of informed and involved worshipers, but our corporate worship has also been enriched by the creativity and gifts of many members.

In 1971, after various attempts to involve more persons proved only temporarily successful, the congregation decided to move its Sunday evening program to Wednesday night. Participation tripled immediately and has continued to grow each year. A cafeteria-style meal forms the axis around which revolves a full afternoon and evening of activities for all ages. At least once a month, and more frequently at Christmas and Easter, worship for all ages brings the entire church family together.

The diaconate continues to assist in pastoral ministry and overall spiritual leadership. Deacon visitation with the members has been active since 1962. Training sessions aimed at developing ministry skills are held regularly and since 1977 two monthly diaconate meetings each quarter are set aside for in-depth sharing with deacon ministry groups. Women were ordained as deacons in 1971 and the first woman chairperson was elected in 1973. Teams of deacons have shared our church's pilgrimage at weekend renewal conferences in churches in Virginia and Illinois. The semi-annual diaconate retreats have been the source of a number of the creative processes that have affected the church: the original study group, the year-long goal study, a retreat study committee, and a long range planning committee.

Small groups play an important part in our church life. From 1967 until 1970, growth groups led by staff and other members used the Yokefellow's spiritual growth tests to focus upon personal growth and the nurturing of Christian community. Since then, the emphasis has shifted to short-term groups formed around specific concerns: parent effectiveness training, grief groups (offered twice yearly), parents of teens, the middle years, and marriage enrichment. Groups have also been offered for specific ages (teens, retirees, young adults) and special needs (recently separated and divorced, problems of aging parents, newly married, the single parent). Ongoing groups include adult and youth weekday Bible studies and an intercessory prayer group. Retreats at the church and away from Vienna also provide experiences in Christian community. Annual camps for children and youth are held as well as retreats for the diaconate, church council, junior high, high school and college youth, women of the church, and choirs.

Adult Sunday School classes use both denominational curriculum and topical studies. Such a varied offering is possible only because of the many resource people in the congregation and larger metropolitan community.

Additional full-time and part-time staff positions have provided resource persons for changing ministries of the church. Beginning in 1976, Vienna Baptist Church entered into an internship relationship with Southeastern Baptist Theological Seminary in Wake Forest, North Carolina. A student spends a year serving as a pastoral associate under supervision of the church staff. Although responsibilities mainly include ministry with youth, the intern is exposed to the full range of church life and pastoral ministry.

The church's approach to the stewardship of possessions has been one of continual emphasis on proportionate giving. Members are confronted with needs and projected programs, but an annual budget is not drawn up until the congregation has pledged for the coming year. In 1978, 575 resident members gave $185,000 through the church.

One dominant lesson from our experiences at Vienna is that the church is always a pilgrim people in process. The journey is always changing and "successful" ministries are to be celebrated but not set in concrete.

We are learning that, above all else, we are called to be a community of Christ's people, open to each other and the Spirit who creates the church. In a few years our community has changed from being almost exclusively a typical single-family residential area to include townhouses and apartments. Young singles, the separated and divorced, the aged, young couples, and college students now join family units in needing our ministry.

The combination of an active black First Baptist Church in Vienna and ethnic Vietnamese and Korean church groups meeting in two neighboring Baptist churches (there are five other Southern Baptist churches within a fifteen-minute drive of Vienna) has limited the racial diversity of the church. We do have black, Chinese-American and Spanish-American members, however, and their numbers will probably increase.

We are just moving beyond seeing ourselves as mainly a family-centered congregation. The new Washington, D.C., subway soon will have a terminal three blocks from our church surrounded by a large area zoned for high density development. Larger, more expensive homes continue to be built in the rolling Fairfax County countryside near us. The diversity of the people to whom we are called to minister is becoming more so!

A long range planning committee, with guidance from state Baptist staff, is now using materials prepared by the Metropolitan Missions Department of the Home Mission Board.

The church is blessed with capable lay leaders, many of whom have lived in various parts of our nation. We are also in a county with one of the highest per capita incomes (and costs of living!) in the nation. Such personal and material resources offer challenging opportunities for creative ministry. Despite frequent renovations, overcrowding of our buildings is a problem and a nearby private school is being used on Sundays. The long range planning committee will evaluate this situation in the light of changes in space for future ministries, the need for retreat facilities, the most responsible use of financial resources, the relative merits of new construction versus multiple, and more efficient use of present buildings and rental facilities.

Though we have ventured forth into some significant and exciting ministries, a church is always tempted to play it safe. Vienna Baptist Church has now established a sense of its own identity and a steady stream of members is attracted to our style of being church.

We could simply live off the past—for awhile. But to do so would betray our vision of the church as the pilgrimage of a servant people, covenanted with God and each other, on mission to the world in which we live. This is a vision born of prayer and worship, risk and conflict, success and failure. We have paid a price for it. I pray that we will be true to it in the future.

12.
New Hope Baptist Church
Anchorage, Alaska
William B. Lyons, Pastor

The Reverend Dr. William Lyons is a native of Burnwell, Alabama. In 1965 he retired from the U.S. Air Force after twenty years service. He has been the pastor of New Hope since 1966. He received the Doctor of Divinity degree in 1974 from the Mississippi Baptist Seminary, Jackson, Mississippi. Lyons has been on the Alaska State Parole Board for eight years, and served as chairman. He is the current president of the Alaska Baptist Convention, SBC. Several members of his congregation helped in compiling the information for this case study, especially Janice Burgess.

New Hope Baptist Church is a New Testament Church. As such, we strive to be an organized body of baptized believers equal in rank and privileges, administering our affairs under our recognized head—Christ. We are united in our belief of what he taught and have convenanted together to do what he has commanded.

At New Hope the congregation participates in the sermon almost as much as the pastor does. This interaction between the pulpit and the people makes the service an event that involves the total person in worship. We attempt to feed both the heart and the head. It requires a great deal of effort by the black pastor to bring these two factors together, but to have an authentic service in the best tradition of the black church, such is necessary.

Our history began in 1960 when the church was formally organized by Rev. Ernest Smith. After Smith's death in 1963, Rev. Boyd Rodgers served as pastor. I became New Hope's third pastor in 1966 when I was called from Fairbanks. To meet the demands of a growing church, work began on the enlargement of the education facilities and the sanctuary. This was completed in 1978. Our church is a member of the Southern Baptist Convention, cooperating through the Alaska State Convention and local association. We now have eight hundred enrolled members, most of them black.

Anchorage's topographical and climatic setting greatly determines the work of the church. Anchorage, bounded by mountains on three sides and water on the fourth, has severe, cold winters with long hours of darkness. The Alaskan winters often produce a psychological reaction in many people classified as "cabin fever." The person affected feels caged, overwhelmed, depressed, and lonely.

Another physical limitation with psychological consequences is the distance in actual travel time between Alaska and the "lower forty-eight" states. The closest point of contact with the lower states is Seattle, Washington, which is 1,644 nautical miles away—a three-hour flight by jet.

A third consideration that affects our ministry is the fact that Alaska in general, and Anchorage in particular, has always had a highly mobile population. This is due partly to the number of Armed Forces personnal and their families. Many of these families join New Hope and are active contributors to New Hope's program.

At first glance these factors may appear to be overwhelming, yet they have not stymied New Hope's progress. Responding to cabin fever, the physical isolation and the mobility of our population, New Hope maintains a vigorous church program through the winter months. This includes visitation to the sick, imprisoned and shut-in, plus interdenominational programs with other churches, both black and white. This fellowship not only involves the lonely individual, but the total community benefits from people coming together out of differing denominations, races, and cultures. It also helps our members become proud to be called "New Hopers."

New Hope's mobile members are welcomed and find a source of comfort within the church walls which replaces the home they left behind. The rotation of these families every two to four years does take its toll on the church by creating frequent vacuums. However, while the non-permanent residents are at New Hope, they are trained to go back into the world, wherever it may be, to tell others and to help others live better lives.

Because members have good ideas that ought to be presented to the church, we have a church council that hears suggestions.

This body helps newcomers feel they are part of the church from the beginning and also provides older members with an avenue to express their views.

One of the central factors in the life of New Hope Church is our witnessing. I am an evangelistic-minded pastor who exhorts his people to be bold enough to tell the good news about Christ on an eyeball to eyeball basis. I am concerned that a person have a decent home, nice clothes, food, and a job that gives him dignity. I exhort the flock to make the world better, to help people live better lives, and to try to improve minds.

Our church membership has almost doubled in the last few years. The witnessing program is based on the continued development of church members so they see this as part of the basic obligation of every Christian. Involvement in the program is always the result of a personal commitment by individuals. However, through witnessing, one gains a better understanding of himself and also grows closer to the other members who are witnessing.

New Hope employs the team approach in witnessing. The new Christian is paired with a mature Christian who acknowledges that the most fulfilling moments in witnessing are when, as a direct result of one's witness, a person accepts Christ, unites with the church, and is baptized. It is imperative that the new, the young, or the person witnessing for the first time be provided with the counseling, guidance, direction, support, encouragement, and prayer he will need.

Two key questions are asked about each person who joins New Hope: "Where will the individual fit in?" and "How can the individual be best prepared for the task of being involved in seeking the unreached people of Alaska?"

One of New Hope's most successful witnessing thrusts began by encouraging people whenever, wherever, and whoever, to attend Bible study classes. This gave us the biblical basis for our task. Our efforts focused on a revival preceded by two weeks of prayer held in a different home each evening. Certain areas in the community were pinpointed as targets: areas of greatest need, areas where people were unchurched and unchristian, and areas where people were lonely and depressed. Sixty were enrolled the first night and many of them were later baptized.

Often I find myself realizing that pastors need to depend on their people more because (we) can't do it all . . . and I know something a lot of preachers don't know . . . the church can go on without me. I have found that if I assign, ask, appoint or delegate responsibility to my people, they will get the job done. This insight has the utmost importance in accounting for the growth at New Hope Baptist Church. Although there is no question who the pastor is in the sense of being a shepherd, there is room for dialogue and sharing between the staff, members, and me. A committed attitude of sharing the total responsibility of the ministry can be seen in all phases of our activities.

Lay leadership abounds in New Hope. Laypersons lead the Sunday School and music departments. When witnessing teams go out into the community to bring people to Christ, I am one of them just like the other members of the church. As much as anything, this type of shared responsibility is the result of training that the officers and members receive.

New Hope's deacons assist me by caring for the administrative duties of the church, as well as providing ample opportunity for the spiritual growth of individual members. The deacons maintain a close spiritual and personal relationship with me. In addition to meeting each month to develop ideas for the improvement of the church, deacons can be found praying in the pastor's study before every worship service. Deacons and ministers also lead the weekly prayer services on Wednesday night. Pairs of deacons go out weekly to make contact with those in need.

The board of trustees for New Hope has worked hard within the last six years as the need for the upkeep of the church has increased. This board has planned continuously, in conjunction with recommendations from the board of deacons, for the expansion of the church.

We now have a fully graded Sunday School from preschool to adults. Sunday School teachers have been strengthened through in-service training. We also have a vigorous recruiting campaign for new teachers. Deacons have supported the Sunday School and have helped to make it grow. Sunday School growth can also be attributed to the personal commitment of the workers and teachers, some of whom have taught extended sessions. The Sunday School is essential to our overall growth. Our enrollment has increased from 109 members in 1971 to approximately three hundred in 1978.

The outreach program, under the direction of the Sunday School director, initiated the bus ministry. Bus captains telephone and visit riders. This work began with a small bus carrying twenty-one people, usually making two trips. It was planned for only small numbers, but more requests kept coming. A larger bus was purchased by individual members who gave additional money beyond their regular offering.

Our music has maintained the cultural identity of our members and helped our friends from other denominations and racial groups appreciate the music of the black experience. Our considerable success with teenagers is perhaps based upon the ability of the music to fill a cultural void as well as provide self-expression.

"A group of professionals" is an apt description of New Hope's usher board. This group of twenty-three senior ushers and eighteen youth ushers became very professional in 1971 under the leadership of one of the former presidents. This professionalism was developed through constant training and practice. The board now has books to use as guidelines and has become a very precise and proud auxiliary of the church. They are at every service including weddings, funerals, revivals, and services involving extended fellowship with other churches. They have become one of the church's greatest fund raisers, but more importantly, the usher board provides members with another place of service.

Women play a varied role in New Hope's church program as trustees, program directors, teachers, counselors and auxiliary heads, and in prayer and Bible study groups. The women are in charge of worship and devotion services every fifth Sunday, creating a dimension at New Hope unavailable at many other churches.

Of special significance is the person we consider the mother of the church. Hers is a position ascribed with great respect by the body, yet her function is primarily symbolic. The power she exercises is advisory.

Another church auxiliary is the pastoral aid committee who sees to it that the pastor is honored in a special way during holidays and special events.

We have been blessed with a strong fellowship of men known as the Brotherhood who meet regularly for Bible study. This is a hard-working body of men who have come from a broad spectrum of backgrounds.

The mission program is composed of six groups and is one of the largest and most active among Baptist churches in Alaska. The groups are Girls in Action, Acteens, Baptist Single Women, Baptist Young Women and Baptist Women, and Royal Ambassadors.

The deaconesses and ministers' wives enhance their husbands' ministries through counseling and orienting members, visiting with their husbands, and by serving as examples for other members.

Young children in the church learn early that the church provides channels for self-expression. We are obligated to ensure, guide, direct, and enlighten them to a knowledge of serving God. A smooth transition from spiritual childhood to spiritual maturity is enhanced by:

1. A vigorous and growing Sunday School and Vacation Bible School.

2. Children's and junior choirs, for children five through twelve and for teenagers thirteen through eighteen; the children's choir sings during the morning worship service one Sunday per month and the teenagers sing each Sunday.

3. Junior ushers serve one Sunday a month.

4. Junior deacons are teenagers who are in an internship program for the deaconship. Each second Sunday they are given the same devotional responsibilities as other trained deacons, including the deacon visitation program that week.

5. Junior church instructs how to function effectively as members of an organized church body. Conducted by the youth minister, the service is for children six through twelve.

6. Youth Bible study meets once a week for teenage peer study,

with a focus on teenage problems.

We are presently engaged in planning more adequately for future needs. Some of our emerging plans are (not in a determined order):

- Enlarge our building or buy property to build a new one.
- Organize another satellite church.
- Provide a day care center.
- Start a Christian day school for ages six through eighteen.
- Open a media center of books, tapes, films, etc.
- Place a preacher in Africa.
- Baptize ten percent more people each year.
- Double Cooperative Program contributions.
- Ensure that any child in the congregation who wants to go to college will not be denied because of lack of funds.

We feel that our denomination can be of greater help to churches like ours than in the past. For instance more scholarships for black ministerial students to theological schools should become available. Also it appears to me that the Southern Baptist Convention is not publishing enough literature which accurately depicts the racial and cultural makeup of the minority members of our denomination. The literature needs to provide models reflective of black churches— models that will speak to black churches.

In addition, there is a crying need for encouragement and active recruitment of black and other ethnic and racial minorities willing to dedicate and commit their lives to work on a foreign mission field. Minorities should be encouraged to apply for missionary assignments abroad.

New Hope is located in a highly transient suburban area of Anchorage where many people live in single-family homes and apartment buildings. It is a good place to live and serve regardless of the rapid changes around us. Basically what we have done is to take the programs designed by the various agencies of the Southern Baptist Convention, adapt them to fit our needs, and put them to work. Our opportunities seem to be unlimited and we are excited. We are doing our best to be a faithful church for our Savior.

13.
Lee Road United Methodist Church
Taylors, South Carolina
A. Mickey Fisher, Pastor

Mickey Fisher was born in the small cotton mill village of Buffalo, South Carolina. He is a graduate of Wofford College and Duke Divinity School. Fisher has a strong interest in the impact of urbanization processes on persons and communities. From 1974 to 1978 he served actively as an officer in the Southeastern Jurisdiction Urban Workers Network. He and his wife, Marilyn, are the parents of a son and a daughter.

This study documents the passage of one suburban congregation from birth to crisis to renewal. It is a case study of transition from "new suburbia" to "old suburbia."

Lee Road United Methodist Church is located in Taylors, a community adjacent to Greenville, South Carolina. Lee Road was a child of the 1950s church extension movement. During that decade great numbers of people were moving into new suburban developments where there were no churches. Denominational mission boards rightly perceived this as an evangelistic opportunity and marshaled resources for planting congregations.

The beginning of Lee Road Church was at a meeting of nine persons in the home of Reverend D. W. Smith on February 9, 1958. Three months later Lee Road was organized with thirty-one charter members. In five years there were 256 members; in ten years, 482 members; in fifteen years, 653 members; in twenty years 767 members.

Smith moved to the Lee Road community after his retirement in 1956. An experienced church organizer, Smith recruited a cadre of proven lay leaders to get things moving. The first church school superintendent had held that office twelve years in his former church. The chairman of the first three building committees was a trustee with many years of service in his former church.

After a month of meeting in the Smith home, increased attendance necessitated a move to a store building. Five months after
organization, ground was broken for the first building consisting
of a worship and fellowship hall, a kitchen and seven classrooms.
In another nine months four additional classrooms were added.
Thirty-eight months later, construction was underway on a sanctuary.
In five years Lee Road occupied buildings which are now valued
at $529,000.

Not only did buildings come quickly, but so did organizations
and ministries. While still meeting in the Smith home, a Women's
Society of Christian Service was organized. A Sunday School was
started in a store building and a men's club was organized. Even
before the young church had a building of its own, it was contributing
to the support of a community center across town and sharing in
the mission outreach of its denomination.

After five years D. W. Smith was succeeded by another retired
pastor, Reverend B. B. Black. He had served as a district superintendent and had the skills to lead through the period of stabilization.
This meant continuing to attract new members, getting the building
debt under control, and providing housing for future pastors.

B. B. Black served for four years and left Lee Road as an almost
clinical example of the stabilization stage. The church was flexible
and outgoing toward the community. It was growing in members
and finances. Enthusiasm was high.

The church and the community were attracting people on their
way up the social and economic ladder. Many families came to
the Lee Road area from various textile mill villages in the county
to this more affluent neighborhood.

This migration took place in the late 1950s and early 1960s, a
time when prevailing cultural values reinforced identification with
the church. These new suburbanites were the benefactors of the
1950s prosperity and brought with them positive attitudes and expec-
tations of the church. In the textile villages the church occupied
a central place. So, in new suburbia, the church was assumed to
be important.

Formalism is a time of turning inward, a stage in which a church becomes preoccupied with its own life. For Lee Road it came during a period of rapid community development.

In 1967 Lee Road welcomed Reverend Allen Long as pastor. At that time the church was viewed as a well established, growing church. Major industrial expansion in the 1960s broadened the county's economic base and brought in waves of suburbanites. They came as managers, engineers, and production people.

By 1963 Lee Road's buildings were in place to attract and serve the newcomers. Contacting and cultivating prospective members dominated the time and energies of both lay and clergy leaders. Constant movement in and out of the community created a revolving-door situation with the membership rolls.

Most available resources were focused on keeping up with the people, but community needs were not totally neglected. During this period Lee Road participated in the creation of Greenville Urban Ministry, supported the Taylor's Neighborhood Center, and contributed to the Taylor's Child Development Center.

In 1971, a gymnasium was completed which provided a significant resource for ministry. But the rules for its use make it very clear that the church had turned inward:

1. The use of the multi-purpose building will be restricted to Lee Road United Methodist Church groups or church affiliated groups by invitation. (Exception to this to be approved by committee.)

2. The multi-purpose building will be locked at all times when not properly supervised by committee members, or on approval of church staff.

3. Anytime the multi-purpose building is open, a member of the committee must be present.

4. Guests (are allowed) only at department times and must be prospective members. Overnight and house guests of members will be permitted.

These rules are clearly rules of a church turning inward. The gymnasium provided a great asset for ministering to the community, but rather than invest in staff and program for that purpose Lee Road made double payments on the mortgage!

A church is in the crisis stage of its life cycle when its community begins to change racially, economically, or socially. Lee Road, like most churches, moved into this stage without realizing it. When I succeeded Long as pastor in 1973, there was little awareness that the dynamics contributing to growth had changed.

Land for residential development became scarce. New families continued to come into the county, but to areas several miles from Lee Road. Traffic patterns changed. Four and six lane expressways bypassed the church. Families moving into the subdivisions beyond Lee Road no longer had to drive past the church in their daily travels. Commercial and industrial encroachment threatened the immediate community, lessening its attraction as a place of residence. A large public housing apartment complex went up across the street from the church. Many houses on the street with the church building became rental units and numerous houses in adjacent subdivisions no longer had their original owners.

In a short time, Lee Road's immediate community changed from "new suburbia" to "old suburbia," from a community attracting those on the way up the social and economic ladder to a community attracting those more oriented to survival. This change was first noted in the pastor's "State of the Church Report" dated December 16, 1974:

Since the time of our organization, we have enjoyed a geographical advantage. We have been the most convenient Methodist Church in Greenville's most rapidly growing area. This is no longer true. There is little land left for residential development . . . . The new growth is beyond the Lee Road area and new traffic patterns bypass East Lee Road. A high percentage of the homes around us already have their second owners. Some have become rental houses.

Future growth will not be easy for Lee Road. If we are not prayerful and thoughtful in our planning and in our working, our strength and vitality can be lost in fewer years than it took to build it.

That same report admonished the church to take missions seriously, continue to work for a high level of excellence in programs, be attentive to the immediate community, landscape and beautify buildings and grounds, begin to think of Lee Road as a "working parish" rather than as a "growing church." Specific proposals for attending to the community included effective visitation, weekday ministries for youth, aggressive recruitment for the church school, monitoring requests for zoning changes, and strong support of public schools.

The 1975 "State of the Church Report" confirmed the negative impact of community change. Statistical comparisons from that report are shown below.

MEMBERS

Added:	1974	1975
Profession of faith	11	15
Transfer from other UMC	59	41
Transfer from other denominations	3	10
TOTAL ADDED	73	66
Removed:		
Death	0	3
Transferred to other UMC	23	33
Transferred to other denominations	6	4
Total REMOVED	29	40
Net Gain:	44	26
Full Members at End of Year	723	697
AVERAGE ATTENDANCE		
Morning worship	296	281
Sunday School	293	262
BUDGET FUND RAISED	$89,475	$98,227

Declining growth rate, decreasing attendance, an alarming gap between membership and participation—such data called for decision.

To speak of Lee Road's journey toward renewal is not to claim the church has arrived. It is to say that we became aware of change in the community, intentionally set some goals and moved in a particular direction. A decision was made by the council on ministries and the administrative board to minister to the community.

The decision to serve the community was grounded in two convictions: (1) that it was God's will and (2) that it was the surest way to preserve Lee Road's strength and assure the future. These convictions still stand. If significant numbers of the survival-oriented people in the community are attracted, the church is likely to find it more difficult, but not impossible, to attract the upward striving people within and beyond the community. Trauma may be ahead. But the hope is that early detection and quick response can make renewal less painful.

Lee Road is not setting the world on fire, but efforts at renewal have not yet produced a losing numbers game. In 1977 membership reached a high of 806; sixty-two were removed for nonparticipation, and by June of 1978 it was back to 767. The decline in worship attendance has been reversed. It was 281 in 1974, 303 in 1977, and 310 in 1978. The decline in Sunday School attendance has been arrested but not reversed. It was 262 in 1974, 264 in 1977. The budget has increased from $81,528 in 1973 to $130,543 in 1978.

The journey toward renewal began with failure. 1974 was designated the year of "The Big Step Forward" in mission and ministry. A director of Christian education joined the staff. But net growth in members was less than the previous year. That failure resulted in a closer look at the community.

An evangelistic thrust into the public housing complex near the church was cancelled when it was discovered the people there were being over evangelized by students from a local fundamentalist school and by churches operating bus ministries. It had reached the point of parking lot squabbling over territorial rights by drivers from competing churches. That an evangelism program was planned for people who were being hounded by evengelists dramatized just how much the church was out of touch with community needs.

To become more aware of what was happening, the Greenville Urban Ministry staff was called in to conduct a workshop on local mission response. This was perhaps the beginning of the long journey. Two other events in 1974 figured in early efforts to move from an inward orientation to a community orientation: (1) Black preachers brought the Sunday morning sermon on two occasions, and (2) the buildings were opened to a new Catholic congregation for their weekly services.

In 1975 a young family from Boston moved into the public housing complex. They brought their children to Sunday School and joined the church. Shortly afterward the husband called for an appointment. Some of the children and young people in his building had had a run-in with the police. He wanted to know if the church was willing to work with them. The result was a meeting of the children with the pastor, director of Christian education, and church lay leader. At that meeting an agreement was reached:

1. Lee Road would open the gymnasium two afternoons a week for neighborhood children and youth.

2. The kids would be accountable for the building and clean it up after each use.

3. Lee Road would not look down on them as "those poor kids from Hampton Hall."

4. They did not have to come to Sunday School in order to use the gym.

This agreement symbolized widening concern for the social as well as religious needs of the community.

1976 was the year for intentionally getting started on the journey. The theological statement adopted by the administrative board was:

We at Lee Road point to the basin and towel used by Jesus in washing his disciples' feet as a sign that his church is meant to be a servant community. We understand the church to be much more than well-intentioned people doing good works. The church is more. It is those who accept Jesus Christ as Lord and seek to respond as the Body of Christ to God's activity in the world. As the church we do not ask, "What good can we do?" Rather, "What is God doing and how can we share in his divine activity in our midst?" In answer to this question, we affirm:

A. God is working in our time to heal the hurt of his suffering people;

    B. God is working in our time to break down the barriers that separate his children from one another;

    C. God is working in our time to establish his church as a community of worshiping, caring, serving, and witnessing people.

Among the goals adopted in response to God's healing work were:

1. Care for parents and children in child abuse cases by educating our people regarding the need for foster parents in Greenville County, recruiting volunteers to serve in the "friend-to-friend" program of the Children's Protective Services, offer a meeting place to a Parent's Anonymous group and determine the need for child care in the Lee Road community.

2. Provide an alternative to boredom and delinquency for children in the neighborhood immediately around Lee Road through a program of week-day recreation, utilizing Howard Hall (the gymnasium) and the church grounds.

3. Develop a face-to-face involvement with people in a disadvantaged neighborhood to help them to help themselves through the Greenville Urban Ministry's Block Partnership program.

4. Extend pastoral care and counseling ministries to those in need in the community who are not Lee Road members.

5. Maintain a Good Samaritan Fund for responding to crisis in the church and community.

In addition, the goals adopted in response to God's reconciling work were:

1. The formation of a task group . . . to seek dialogue with the pastor and lay leaders of St. Matthew and St. Mark Churches (neighboring black churches) to communicate our desire to share with them fraternal visits, joint training events, pulpit exchanges, and youth and children's programs.

2. Continue to be gracious hosts to the Prince of Peace congregation (the Catholic Church).

3. To celebrate our unity in Christ through joint services with the Prince of Peace congregation on Ash Wednesday, Passover, Thanksgiving Eve, and the Sunday before Christmas.

4. Establish lines of communication with community leaders in the area immediately around the church—Burns Grocery, Hampton Hall Apartments, Merry Oaks Apartments, school principals and counselors, child care centers, etc.

5. Promote conversation with local government leaders on issues relative to the Bicentennial, election year, and the general health of the community.

1976 was notable, not because of record accomplishments, but because of the clear choice of direction. Lee Road leaders declared their support of the church as an inclusive fellowship open to and caring for the community.

There are no dramatic successes in the Lee Road story. The community has not been radically changed. There has been no great influx of survival-oriented people into the church. There is, however, a greater identity with the community, more openness to the people of the community, and an enlightened commitment to serve the community.

Communication links have been established with community leaders and government agencies. A task group met with the County Planning Commission, secured census track information and long range transportation plans, became familiar with zoning laws, and successfully opposed a zoning change from residential to commercial. Study committees and other groups have met with officers from the Department of Social Services, Children's Bureau, Mental Health Center, County Supervisor's office, and law enforcement agencies. Members of the council on ministries and administrative board have appeared before County Council, County Recreation Commission, County Housing Authority, and the County School Board. Several members have served on citizens' advisory committees for local schools. Dialogue has been established with school principals and counselors, store operators, apartment managers, landlords, and realtors. Candidates for public office have been invited to speak, a reception was held for a new high school principal, and the gymnasium was offered for a "town hall" meeting. The church lawn is used for a Little League practice field and neighborhood sandlot games.

Lee Road's commitment to serve the community has been expressed through pastoral care, child advocacy, recreation, and community organization. The pastor's study was made available to a chaplain from the local hospital system for Monday evening counseling sessions which served the community as well as the church. A child advocacy task group was successful in influencing public policy decisions, in sensitizing school personnel to abused children, and in having Lee Road designated as the site for community parenting workshops.

An afternoon recreation program named for the Hampton Hall children and youth provides craft activities, music, games, conversation, and refreshments for neighborhood children and youth. It is staffed by Lee Road's director of Christian education, adult and youth volunteers from the church, and Furman University students who work through Furman's Collegiate Educational Service Corps. The agreement negotiated with the Hampton Hall kids still stands, though a goal is to win them over to taking part in the regular church program. This is undertaken with a conscious intention to keep the welcome mat out for those who say no to further identification with the church.

Lee Road is in the second year of a Block Partnership, a community organization program under the auspices of the Greenville Urban Ministry. Through this partnership Lee Road and the Prince of Peace parish support the self-improvement efforts of a disadvantaged community two miles from the church. The two churches do not do things for the partnership community. They help the residents to identify needs, set goals, and organize to work toward meeting the goals. The partnership lists these achievements: a door-to-door survey of needs, semi-annual community clean-up days, securing a sanitation dumpster, the removal of condemned housing, frequent recreation and field day events, and four basketball teams. Efforts are focused on lobbying the County Recreation Commission and County Council for a park in the area.

In conclusion, perhaps it is appropriate to mention some lessons that have come to us as a result of living through the process of change:

- Change in suburbia is quicker and less apparent but no less dramatic in its impact on the church than change in the central city.
- Early diagnosis is essential to effective remedy.

- Renewal is a theological task: the church must embrace an inclusive view of church, accept the yoke of servanthood, and understand evangelism as more than soul-saving.
- Suburban lifestyles and values exist in tension with Christian lifestyles and values, creating resistance to renewal.
- Membership care and community concern rank as equals in any workable strategy of renewal: aggressive recruiting of members and nurturing and shepherding care of all members are as necessary as developing programs to serve the community.
- The motives of lay and clergy leaders must be clearly grounded in the gospel.

14.
Middlebelt Baptist Church
Inkster, Michigan
C. E. Martin, Pastor

Rev. C. E. Martin was born in Springfield, Tennessee. He is the son and grandson of Baptist preachers. He holds the Bachelor of Science degree from Tennessee State University and the Bachelor of Divinity degree from the American Baptist Theological Seminary in Nashville. Rev. Martin has served as a pastor in Tennessee, Illinois, and Michigan. He is married and has two sons.

Inkster is a suburb of Detroit. Some forty-two thousand people live in Inkster, but most work in Detroit. The economic base of the community is supported basically by real property assessment as it is 70 percent residential, 20 percent commercial, and only 9 percent industrial. The most important industry has been the manufacturing of transportation equipment.

The majority of the residents are wage earners with steady incomes. However, recent U.S. Department of Commerce studies indicate that 27.5 percent of the population do receive some form of public assistance income.

Inkster was composed almost exclusively of white, middle-class citizens until a few years ago. Racial tension and riots in Detroit near the end of the 1960s saw fear and panic erupt all over the greater metropolitan area. Inkster was caught up in swift racial change. Now the community contains 51 percent white and 49 percent black residents. Most of the families own their homes and demonstrate pride in maintaining their property.

Middlebelt Baptist Church was started in the summer of 1957 as a Southern Baptist mission sponsored by the Merriman Baptist Church of Garden City, Michigan. On the first Sunday, twenty-five individuals met for Bible study and worship in a commercial building just beyond the city limits of Detroit. The first pastor was Rev. Asa Hunt. The small group constituted into a church November 27.

A year later the church moved to a farm house with a sizable tract of land on Middlebelt Road. Numerical growth was increasing steadily and a decision was made in the early 1960s to build an educational facility which was completed in 1963.

On March 27, 1966, the congregation voted to erect a larger sanctuary. It was built and dedicated one year later. The membership of the church continued to increase and a full agenda of programs and activities for all ages was developed. By 1971 the members numbered 641 and the total receipts for the year were $53,546.

But the racial status of the community was changing from predominantly white to black and other ethnic groups. Members of the church began to sell their property and move. Many of them transferred their membership to churches farther away from Detroit. The growth that Middlebelt church had enjoyed for its brief history soon stopped and decline became evident.

The tensions displayed in the community were felt in the church. The first black family, the James Hamiltons, joined the congregation on April 26, 1974. Hamilton was placed on the usher committee. The church continued to lose members and the next year the pastor resigned. Blacks were visiting the church but were not joining and the pastor was frustrated about it. As of 1975 the young church had been served by ten pastors.

The Martin family moved to Inkster from Romulus, Michigan, in 1975, and became the second black family to join Middlebelt Baptist Church. At the time I was employed by the government. Shortly thereafter I was asked by the congregation to become the interim pastor. Two months later I was called as the full-time pastor. I realized that a large percentage of the church activities and programs had grown weak. Many members were discouraged and indifferent. Some hoped a black pastor would help to reach the changing community, but others were not pleased that I had come.

To increase Sunday School and children's church attendance, the bus ministry was reactivated. However, the Sunday School workers had not been prepared for the influx of minority children and tension increased. Soon Sunday School attendance declined and the children's church worship hour was discontinued. At the same time, increasing numbers of blacks were joining the church.

Several of the leaders thought that the less said about race, the smoother the function of the church would be. The conclusion by some was that the prejudices of the past should not be mentioned and activities should be operated without discussing the factors necessary for blacks and whites to work together as a team. Yet, as time went by, conflict increased.

Music became a point of tension. A few black members wanted an all-black choir. Some white members stopped singing in the adult choir because they could not sing the blacks' style.

When an interracial couple visited the church and inquired about membership, the prejudices of both groups came to the surface. Without investigation some accusations were made about the couple. One man stated that it was all he could do to accept blacks as members in the first place, but he could not tolerate this! The couple eventually was accepted as members, but because of the lack of social acceptance the white woman returned to her former church and the boyfriend no longer attends anywhere. As a result of the situation some white members left the church declaring that there was no Christian love at Middlebelt and that the church was more interested in worldy matters than soul-winning. Some blacks and whites simply did not believe in mixing the races for dating and marriage. One deacon left the church in protest.

Other problems have arisen as a result of church traditions. A portion of the white members wanted the church to be organized strictly according to Southern Baptist customs and procedures. Several of the blacks insisted that the church be operated as they had been accustomed to in their former National Baptist congregations. The whites were afraid that the blacks would take over the church, and the blacks were afraid that the whites would control everything.

It became apparent that before a church can reach and work with a racially changing community, the members need to face up to themselves. When the Sunday School workers are not spiritually prepared for transition, effective teaching is not possible. When the deacons do not understand the purpose of the church, confusion takes place. When the church council is not sensitive to the spiritual and emotional needs of the members, hurt feelings arise.

Upon recognizing that our basic problems were more from within than from without, I began to change my methods of leadership. I had thought that what we needed most urgently were new members. Instead we needed to first work on ourselves. We had to acknowledge our own prejudices and seek biblical alternatives such as Galatians 3:26-28: "For ye are all the children of God by faith in Christ Jesus. For as many of you as have been baptized into Christ have put on Christ. There is neither Jew nor Greek, there is neither bond nor free, there is neither male nor female, for ye are all one in Christ Jesus."

We have found at Middlebelt that there is no desire to change for the better when individuals do not see an attitude or an action as wrong. So in relation to our traditional thoughts and prejudices, biblical change is being sought. However, biblical change does not take place without repentance.

I have resorted primarily to preaching and teaching the basic principles of the gospel. Consistent emphasis has been placed on God's priorities and the needs of the community. Business meetings have been devoted to working on internal matters. Hours have been spent with deacons and organizational leaders to discuss the conflicts as well as the opportunities of the church for advancement.

The Sunday School staff includes black and white directors and teachers. Regular training meetings have been started again. We emphasize lesson plans, and personal contact with people who missed the previous Sunday. A great deal of attention is given to helping the Sunday School leaders adjust their literature and teaching methods to provide relevant information and guidance for people in a transitional community. We use books, conferences, evaluation sessions, associational meetings, or whatever it takes to upgrade our Sunday School.

Major attention has been given to the Woman's Missionary Union of the church. Much of the WMU program has been traditional Southern Baptist and this has caused tension. White women work effectively in certain aspects of missions whereas, traditionally, black women have had Bible lessons, have worked in special ways to help the church financially, have sought to meet local missionary needs, and have done personal witnessing. Some of the tension has come when the emphasis has been foreign mission concerns away from the immediate community.

I am working with the WMU leaders to make the women of the church aware of the Southern Baptist program, as well as use every opportunity to reach a changing community. The WMU director and two other women attended Ridgecrest Baptist Conference Center in North Carolina to learn more about the Southern Baptist Bold Mission Thrust. A white woman is the president of the WMU and a black woman is the president of the Baptist Women. Some work is being done to involve girls in missions. One setback has been lack of women leaders to do the work.

The director of the Baptist Men and financial secretary of the church is a black man who is learning the structure of the men's work among Southern Baptists. This organization was started during the summer of 1978. Men are being prepared to work with the boys, become involved in the care of the building, learn the basic work of the Brotherhood, invite other men to church and to salvation in Christ, and urge indifferent Christian men to accept the responsibilities of church membership.

Pastoral counseling is another medium that has assisted our members. Through intense counseling sessions a better rapport has been established between pastor and people as personal prejudices have been faced in the light of biblical teachings.

In my estimation, the main setback to our growth as a church has not been racial prejudice altogether. Family problems have been the primary hindrance. As families are helped, they are urged to reach out and support other families in trouble, and we are seeing this happen.

The conditions within our church are not the best by any means, but they are getting better. I am convinced that the honest confrontations and counseling appointments have helped greatly. Our people are becoming more willing to take the time to talk about their problems, fears, and hurts. Many are realizing that their attitudes and words are often a detriment to the work of the church and that they must repent and accept the direction of the Holy Spirit.

The deacon's family ministry plan has been introduced to the church. Training classes have been held for the deacons and they have read helpful materials. Families and single persons have been assigned to the deacons for watchcare. More and more the pastor is referring certain persons to the deacons for ministry. We now have black and white deacons. In 1978 a very meaningful retreat was held with the deacons concerning the spiritual growth and development of the church.

To help with the practical needs of everyday living, I lead a Bible class each Wednesday to help the members learn how to use the Scriptures in relation to life's problems. Attention has been centered also on the prayer life of the Christian.

At Middlebelt we have tried to challenge our members to zero in on the particular needs of the congregation and the community so that people, regardless of race, can be reached for Christ. Consequently, we try to blend the talents of everybody so as to develop each person's potential. Great care is given to placing an individual in a position of responsibility so that person's gift can be enhanced.

Much time and attention has been directed toward worship services. Hymns published by both blacks and whites are being sung. White members are being taught the use of black music in order to enrich the worship experience, and blacks are learning to appreciate unfamiliar hymns generally sung by whites. The music selected for worship consists of a variety of hymns, gospel songs, spirituals, anthems, solos, duets, and instrumentals. Gradually black and white worship styles have blended to maintain the interest and increase the worship for everyone.

Also, the purpose and specific use of the offering is explained in the context of worship to avoid "milking" the congregation.

The preaching of the gospel at Middlebelt is practical—for everyday living. The members are factory workers, teachers, coaches, housewives, law enforcement officers, and retired persons. Most are under fifty-five years of age and are young Christians, seeking answers to pressing problems. We define worship as a special experience with God that results in personal growth and Christian activity. Hence, our worship services are designed for that special time with God—in spite of one's situation—so that the person can deal more effectively with his life and the world after the benediction is pronounced.

We are beginning to witness some positive results in terms of outreach into the community. The Sunday School is growing again, especially the adult men's and women's classes and the children's groups. New people are coming. The women of the church have started a crisis closet to help families get adequate food and clothing.

For the first time in several years more new members were gained in 1978 than lost. The racial make-up of the congregation is about 30 percent black and 70 percent white of the active members with a total membership of 544. Average attendance for Sunday morning worship is around two hundred and is often half white and half black. A noticeable increase in attendance has been occurring for the Sunday evening services.

We have developed a strategy for evangelism which consists of eighteen people divided into five groups. They volunteered for this work and were trained. Each group has a particular responsibility such as (1) recruiting and equipping additional evangelistic witness teams, (2) contacting new residents in the community, (3) talking with non-Christians in the Sunday School about their own salvation, (4) visiting in the homes of those persons who are visitors to the church worship services and also contacting inactive church members, and (5) keeping up-to-date evangelistic records for evaluation and referral.

Members of Middlebelt can be found quite often providing ministries at the Veteran's Hospital, homes for retired persons, and at the Baptist Center in Detroit, and helping to prepare meals for seventy to eighty people in need of hot, nourishing food. During the summer the teenagers conduct backyard Bible clubs for children not in church anywhere.

The congregation is demonstrating a deeper awareness of the need for giving to missions. Each week 13½ percent of the receipts goes to support the missionary endeavors of Southern Baptists. Special offerings go to foreign and home missions. A teenage girl in the church recently has been prayerfully considering service overseas.

The working relationship between pastor, deacons, organizational leaders, and committee members has improved to the extent that more effective results are being observed throughout the total church program. There is a more relaxed and open relationship. The congregation seems to be learning how to communicate in love with each other and with the community. An atmosphere of compassionate care for others is being felt more and more.

It isn't easy to be in a church like Middlebelt. In the midst of steady social change coming from all directions, the pastor and leaders must constantly seek God's direction and guidance to avoid as much conflict as possible. It does increase one's prayer life to be the pastor of such a church!

Every day it seems that new problems arise. Some parents are suspicious that their teenagers might become too friendly with teenagers of another race if the youngsters become greatly involved in youth activities. Sometimes, the teenagers question in anger the depth of their parents' Christian commitment. Hurtful statements are made about whether or not a man or woman should be leading the music during worship services. Some persons let it be known that they are just waiting around for the church to fold up now that it has a black pastor.

My family and I have borne the brunt of some reactions and experiences which are unprintable. Our oldest son has been dismayed and disappointed over the prejudices of some people. Many times my wife and I have turned to the congregation for prayer on behalf of our family.

As to my personal feeling, I do not look upon it as an honor to be the pastor of a predominantly white church. Neither do I look upon it as an honor to be pastor of a black church. According to the Scriptures the church is not to be identified by the racial characteristics of the members. Rather the church is to be identified by an obedient relationship with Jesus Christ.

National Baptists and Southern Baptists have a number of similarities. We do not need to fear each other. We can serve together to reach our communities for Christ. In Michigan we are told that 50 percent of our citizens are not in church anywhere. As Christians we should be marching side by side because of our heritage from Christ instead of dwelling on our white or black heritages so much. There should be no question regarding whose business we are about. If we are about the Father's business, there is going to be a relationship with the Father's children which glorifies him. Then we become our brother's keeper and our brother's brother.

Churches like ours need encouragement and support of all kinds from our denominational agencies, seminaries, and stronger churches. We must have workers and money and training conferences. Our priorities must become the concern of our leaders. We know now that we can reach people in a transitional area and we need support in doing our work.

To me the appointment to Middlebelt is another opportunity for Christ to be glorified. In the words of Paul in Philippians 4:11-13: "I have learned in whatsoever state I am therewith to be content. I know both how to be abased, and I know how to abound: everywhere and in all things I am instructed both to be full and to be hungry, both to abound and to suffer need. I can do all things through Christ which strengtheneth me." I am more grateful than ever that I was saved by grace and called into the ministry.

A pastor of a church in a changing community can feel gratitude when he sees Christ glorifying himself through that pastor's spiritually delegated leadership. After a few years have gone by and the church clerk reports that the number of new members is greater than the loss, the pastor knows that Christ is glorifying himself. When members say that the church is not pressured as much by finances and debt retirement; when visitation is gaining; when the fellowship of the church is becoming more loving; when the spiritual growth of individuals is obvious; then the pastor knows that Christ is glorifying himself.

I am a witness that a pastor who experiences something like this feels mighty good about his place of service.

15.
Rainbow Park Baptist Church
Decatur, Georgia
Gene Tyre, Pastor

The author of this case study was born in Jesup, Georgia. He has been the pastor of four churches, all in his home state. He is a graduate of Brewton-Parker Jr. College, Mercer University, and the Southern Baptist Theological Seminary in Louisville, Kentucky where he received his Master of Divinity and Doctor of Ministry degrees.

Standing before the congregation were a white couple, a black couple, a woman and her retarded child—all presenting themselves for church membership.

What is there about this church that has enabled it to minister to such a diversity of persons? What role have the staff and laypersons played in developing ministries to meet the needs of persons? What process has the church used in coming to discover its identity? What is the identity of the church now?

This case study will seek to share answers to these questions.

The first meetings of the church were held in a brush arbor a century ago. In its infancy the church was named Beech Springs Baptist Church. In 1894 the name of the church was changed to the Kirkwood Baptist Church, and the name was maintained until 1969 when it was given its present name.

From 1894 until 1969, the church relocated three times. The first two moves were motivated by a need for larger facilities due to a growing congregation. Those moves were within the city of Atlanta. The third move was brought about by the racial change of the community. From 1894 until 1963 the church was a community church with more than 95 percent of the members living within the immediate community.

During this time the church had some outstanding pastors including a former president of the Southern Baptist Convention, K. Owen

White. The church took pride in having the largest Training Union program in the Convention.

In the early 1960s the community began to experience racial transition. The end result was that many church members departed. Church programs, including finances, began to decline.

The church had purchased property in suburban DeKalb County for a new mission. However, when the Kirkwood community experienced racial change, the decision was made to locate the church approximately twelve miles away.

On Sunday, February 2, 1969, the first service was held at what is now known as the Rainbow Park Baptist Church, 2941 Columbia Drive, Decatur, Georgia. The church found itself in a community experiencing tremendous growth. It was surrounded by new single-family and multi-family housing developments. The community was rapidly becoming a part of white middle and upper-middle class suburbia.

Today the church is once again located in a racially integrated community. The community began to experience racial change in 1973—only four years after the church moved to its present location.

The people of our church come from various backgrounds and communities. A recent report reveals that approximately 40 percent of the members live in a three mile radius of the church building. Twenty-four percent live four to six miles from the church. Twelve percent live from seven to ten miles away, and 24 percent live more than ten miles away.

Within a five-mile radius of the church building are houses that range from $25,000 to $100,000.The community is composed of blue collar and white collar workers. The area continues to experience change as blacks and ethnic groups are moving into the community, and whites are moving out.

The church—also composed of persons from different racial and cultural backgrounds—is a microcosm of the community. While the congregation has persons of wealth as well as those on social security, the majority of the members come from the middle class. The average educational level of the adults is one to two years of college.

The membership of the church in 1962 was 2,907. The membership in 1969, the year the church moved to its new facility, was 2,182. One can readily see that in a period of seven years the church lost 725 members. This loss occurred during a period of rapid community change. From the time of relocation in 1969 until 1973 when the community began to experience racial change the membership increased by twenty-eight persons. During this time the community was experiencing tremendous population growth.

Since 1973, again during a time of racial transition, the membership has increased by 111 persons. The church has shown a small increase each year over the past four years.

In September, 1974, I became pastor of the church. I arrived with the knowledge that the church was facing the challenge of ministering to a community in the process of change. Depression was everywhere. Time and again I heard the question, "What are we going to do, since we are now facing and will continue to face the same thing we faced in Kirkwood?" The first months of my ministry were spent listening to persons as they shared their frustrations and their hopes. The sermons that were preached in those early months sounded the theme of hope. I met with deacons and other church leaders individually and in groups. We met in my home and in the homes of the members. These meetings built firm relationships.

Early I discovered that self-identity was a necessity at Rainbow Park. A church council was organized and began to deal with questions such as "Where have we been? Who are we? What is going to be the shape of our ministry?" Attention was given to the church's history, identifying strengths and weaknesses.

Lyle Schaller's book, *Hey, That's Our Church,* was introduced to the council. He identifies the uniqueness of different congregations. This book played a significant part in helping the council understand the identity of Rainbow Park.

Since the congregation is scattered throughout metro Atlanta, and the church had a history of strong involvement in evangelism and missions, Rainbow Park decided not to limit itself to being a neighborhood church. The identity would be a church on mission, located in the suburbs with a city on its heart. The first goal was to call a staff with expertise in urban ministries. A job description was developed which determined the kind of persons needed to help the church maintain its identity as a church on mission.

Recognizing the need for missions in the immediate community, the church called a minister of activities. We owned an activities building but desperately needed a program to go into the building. The minister of activities organized a basketball league for all ages, craft classes, volleyball leagues, skating, golf, slimnastics, backpacking, day camping, and a hunter safety program. The church was able to see immediately the positive impact a Christian recreation program could have upon the church and community. Thus a lighted athletic field and tennis court were developed. The church has eight softball teams and provides facilities for a softball league. This program has provided tremendous exposure for the church. The minister of activities has led others to see that Rainbow Park is on mission and that mission includes a ministry to the total person.

The minister of music rapidly began a program oriented toward missions. The expansion of the children's choir appealed to families who had no other involvement in the church. During the Christmas season choirs and handbell groups hold concerts in shopping centers and subdivisions.

The calling of a minister of education completed the full-time ministerial staff. He has developed a quality Bible study program. A weekday Bible study class meets on Tuesday morning, and plans are to hold Bible studies in nursing homes and other institutions. A youth Bible study is also held during the week. Each year a group of Sunday School officers and teachers attend denominational workshops. It is through Bible study and sharing in small Bible study groups that koinonia is rapidly becoming a reality.

Recently, in order to give our youth someone with whom to identify, a part-time minister of youth was called. Plans are now being made to open a youth center that will house counseling, fellowship, and Bible study.

The commitment of the staff to ministry in an integrated community has positively influenced the church. The hope that radiates from the staff has helped to stabilize the church and community.

In 1972 the church in conference had adopted the following motion (formulated by the deacons): "It is recommended that all people be welcomed at Rainbow Park Baptist Church, without regard to creed, color, or national origin." As the community continued to experience racial change, and as the church began to reach out into the community, blacks began visiting the church.

"What will happen if a black person presents himself for church membership?" some members asked. Thus in 1976 another motion was presented to the church: "Having adopted in 1972 a recommendation from the deacons that all people without regard to race, color, or national origin be welcomed by the church and consistent with its bylaws, this church does hereby reaffirm and declare that race, color, or national origin shall not be a condition of membership, and further that it is the policy and intention of this church to reach persons and minister in the name of Jesus Christ throughout the community."

The church was notified that at a regular church conference this matter would be presented to the people. After presentation of the recommendation, the discussion seemed open and honest. As the discussion was moving toward conclusion, an elderly member of the congregation came forward. He was a man well known throughout the church family. He had operated a grocery store in Kirkwood community for many years, and when community change set in he had been robbed and severely injured. As he limped to the microphone, silence fell over the congregation. He held onto the microphone, and sang, "Jesus loves the little children of the world. Red and yellow, black and white they are precious in his sight, Jesus loves the little children of the world." These words— coming from this particular man—moved the business meeting to an experience of worship.

Immediately the question was called, and the final vote was 184 for the recommendation and thirteen against.

Blacks continued to come, and four months later a black man presented himself for church membership. He was accepted by a unanimous vote of the congregation. The church now has approximately thirty-seven black members, eleven of whom have come on profession of faith. They serve as Sunday School teachers and on key committees.

Bridges of communication are being built among persons of the congregation. Operation Relationship is a ministry provided by the spouses of the deacons. Each person who joins the church is adopted for six weeks by a family within the church. Families come to know one another and new members are introduced to the ministries of the church.

Wednesday night prayer meeting has also been given to the building of a strong fellowship. During the service I conduct an informal, open interview with those who have recently joined the church so we can get to know each other. In these interviews I raise such questions as family background, job, community involvement, the reasons for joining the church, and the highlight of the person's Christian pilgrimage at Rainbow Park.

What about those who have responded negatively to blacks coming into the congregation? Several families left the church. They made their feelings known to friends and church leaders and left without creating a problem.

There are those in the congregation who have difficulty belonging to a church that includes persons of different races. These persons have not been condemned by staff or church.

When they come to ventilate their feelings, they are listened to. Positive changes in the lives of these persons take place with regularity. There are those who have been members of the church for many years who are coming to see that persons of different races desire to be a part of a church that is on mission. Racial tensions are relieved as persons come to know one another. The church continually provides this opportunity.

The church council serves as the administrative arm of the church. The council meets monthly, evaluating ministries and sharing plans. These meetings are characterized with respect for the total ministry of the church. By coordinating the ministries of the church through the church council, scheduling conflicts are kept to a minimum.

The diaconate, one of the real strengths of the church, is given to serving persons in and out of the church.

The diaconate is composed of six ministry teams: hospital visitation, shut-in and bereavement, administration, outreach, new member, and pastor advisory team. The captains of these teams meet with me before each deacons' meeting for reports from the teams. Thus, the congregation views the deacon as a servant. Deacons are always present during worship to assist those who come for church membership. When the new members stand to receive a welcome from the church, a deacon stands with them.

Wednesday night provides a time for fellowship, children's choirs, mission activities, committee meetings, and leadership training. I lead advanced Bible study followed by a time of prayer and sharing. The church is preparing videotapes so the congregation can study with seminary professors and other professionals.

The time of prayer and sharing is most meaningful. Prayer is offered for those who are sick. Shut-ins are mentioned by name. The next morning a card is sent to these persons, telling them that their church remembered them. The meeting concludes when I kneel at the church altar and invite those who desire to join me in asking God's blessing upon the church and its ministries to persons.

Worship services are characterized by dignity, warmth, and variety. Music ranges from anthems to gospel songs. Both Sunday morning and evening worship hours make room for flexibility.

My sermons are expository in nature. A series of sermons on the mission of the church as outlined in the book of Acts enabled the church to see its mission to the community and beyond. The themes of hope and assurance helped us be more aware of God's involvement as we strive to live as the family of God. Sermons also deal with issues which face a changing community, such as racism, politics, and Christian citizenship.

During worship services, laypersons share experiences that have taken place during their Christian pilgrimage.

It is our strong evangelistic tradition that we have been able to build upon. The challenge in recent years has been to develop a model of evangelism that reaches all persons.

Visitation takes place on Thursday night, although many persons fear to visit in an integrated community. But rather than waiting for new families to visit the church, the style is for families within the church family to invite new families in their neighborhood to visit the church.

A class for training witnesses is taught once a year. Attendance is by invitation only and provides an opportune time to deal with fears of relating to persons of different races.

Rainbow Park does not pit evangelism against social ministries. The foundation is evangelism that leads to involvement in the needs of persons.

I feel that it is very important to be involved in local government and community activities. Consequently, I serve on the county mental health advisory committee and the county economic development committee. I was one of the organizers and first president of the South Dekalb Christian Association, a group of clergy and laypersons working together to develop a positive attitude of persons toward the community. I am on the board of directors of Project Read, a tutorial service. I attend county commission meetings and meet at least once a month with the commissioner who serves the immediate community. This enables me to be aware of what is happening throughout the metro area, especially in the church's neighborhood.

I attend literary and athletic events at local schools and am on the board of directors of the Boys Clubs of America. From time to time government officials are invited to participate in our worship services.

The church has joined with the county in a joint ministry to the mentally retarded. The program is called Communitization. Its basic thrust is to move mentally retarded persons from state institutions back into the community. The county pays the rent on a home owned by the church. The church provides food for the clients and counselors, and has developed ministries for the mentally retarded. Recently the church was awarded the Vital Service Award, presented annually by the Atlanta Association for Retarded Citizens.

Our kindergarten helps to meet the needs of children. Those enrolled in this program come from the immediate community.

Through parent meetings and participation by parents in special church events, bridges of communication have been built between black and white.

Some parents were concerned about the quality of education their children were receiving in the public schools. After studying this, the church voted to establish a first grade, adding a grade each year. In the first year of operation, the first grade class included whites, blacks, Spanish, and Orientals. Community response to the school has been tremendous. Families whose only contact with the church had been kindergarten or primary school have turned to the church for ministry in time of need.

Each time the Lord's Supper is observed, a special offering is taken to help those in need. The church operates the Janie Grant Benevolence Center, housed in the church building. The benevolence committee operates a clothes closet and food pantry. But this committee does not wait for the needy to come to our building. If the committee is informed of a need, they visit the home to discuss how the church can serve—from finding temporary housing to paying pharmaceutical bills.

Each year in cooperation with the Atlanta Baptist Association, the church provides a day camp for inner city children. This camp is staffed by senior high youth, and women of the church provide a hot lunch.

Pioneers is the name of a ministry designed for older adults who have a tie to the church that goes back many years. These persons meet once a month to enjoy entertainment or a speaker who can relate to them. They also take out-of-town trips twice a year to points of interest.

To strengthen family ties within the church and community, we host an annual family life conference for all ages that is not limited to our members. Leaders have ranged from a local pastor with expertise in this ministry to the chief clinical chaplain of an outstanding medical school.

On the church calendar is an annual Bible study conference led by a seminary professor. This event is promoted in churches throughout the community, fostering fellowship across denominational lines.

During the summer, contact is made with secularly operated nursery schools and day-care centers, and for one week children from these institutions join children from the church for study and fun at Vacation Bible School. Thus members have worked with children of varied racial and social backgrounds, and have had a learning as well as teaching experience.

The church's mission involvement, built again on tradition, is illustrated by such projects as:

• The salaries of two foreign missionaries are supplemented by the church through the Foreign Mission Board.

• Each summer a group of our young people minister in Atlanta Baptist Association mission centers. Also, they have been instrumental in beginning a church in Strasburg, Pennsylvania, and in strengthening work in Convoy, Ohio, and London, Kentucky.

• Laypersons work at Atlanta's mission centers, conducting Bible study classes and improving the physical facilities. It was a first for the church when a group of men participated in a mission trip to Detroit to instruct church leaders and do lay witnessing.

• The minister of music and I participated in an evangelistic crusade in Idaho which was a joint mission with the Home Mission Board. The church also sent me on a mission trip to South Africa and Kenya, helping to strengthen the ties of the church with foreign missions.

One of our real strengths has occured in the stewardship of finances. When the church relocated in 1969, the budget was $183,139. In 1975 the budget was $355,535. Even though the immediate church community has experienced racial and some economic change, gifts to the church have increased yearly. Since 1969, every mission offering goal has been met.

Through a monthly report, the church finance committee continually makes our people aware of where the money is being used. This report is presented in a positive manner, sharing some of the things that have been accomplished because of the generosity of our members. The staff works with the finance committee in stewardship education through denominational stewardship promotional materials. One of the highlights of the year is an annual stewardship banquet.

The church buildings of Rainbow Park are designed for ministry.

Our complex includes a sanctuary, educational space, and an activities building which houses basketball and volleyball courts, a crafts center, and educational space. The buildings are shared with the community. The county recreation department and the local YMCA have used the church facilities. Local music teachers use the church sanctuary for recitals. Political forums are also held on church property. A local black congregation uses the fellowship hall for its Christmas party each year.

The residents see the church as a vital part of the community. It is this kind of involvement that led a local government leader to declare "Rainbow Park has done more to bring stability to South DeKalb County than any other institution."

Rainbow Park is not only attempting to structure its ministry to meet the needs of today but also tomorrow. In 1977 a long-range planning and survey committee was established to study and determine future ministries. The committee was divided into subcommittees: community profile, building, music, public relations, education, activities, finance, ministries, and evangelism. These subcommittees worked very closely with the staff and reported their findings and recommendations to the church. One of the more significant recommendations was the establishment of a committee responsible for a continuous monitoring of the different ministries. This committee will also evaluate present ministries and recommend new ones as needs surface within the church and community.

The formation of a specialized training class for church leaders, including the use of videotape, will help prepare quality leaders during the years ahead. The long-range planning committee also recommended enlargement of the church fellowship hall and educational space, the development of a radio and television ministry, the church sponsorship of a retirement home, and the acquisition of property for the establishment of a mission church somewhere in the metropolitan community.

The community profile subcommittee enabled the church to come to a realistic view concerning community growth. The report seems to validate the fact that growth of the church will depend upon the church taking itself outside the church building in an aggressive program of evangelism and missions.

In a recent sermon I stated to the congregation that as we view the days and years ahead, what is out in the future is not as important as who is out there. The congregation known as Rainbow Park Baptist Church believes that God is not only involved in the here and now, but he is also out there. He is leading as we struggle, assuring of his presence even when we fail, and lifting when we fall. With that assurance the church faces the future with a strong determination to continue a ministry to the total person in the name of Jesus Christ.

The church cannot accomplish this alone. It needs the support of denominational agencies in reinterpreting the meaning of success in ministry. We need to be told that when the work of the church is completed, the memorabilia of success will not be contained in associational minutes, church budgets, or clippings from denominational papers, but in the lives of individuals. Seminars and sharing groups need to be provided for ministers and their families who live in and are ministering to changing communities for a time of valuable brainstorming.

The seminaries could provide summer interns for churches—a profitable experience for the intern and for the church.

Rainbow Park's ministry has come as a result of establishing an identity. It is a church committed to ministry to a city and the regions beyond. Coming to this identity has increased the vision of the church. The congregation now sees that our future is not going to be determined completely by what happens to the immediate community. We come to the building for equipping and then turn to the world for ministry. The acceptance of this identity has enabled the church to appeal to those who live outside the immediate community. The ability of the church to grow in membership during the past five years while experiencing a community in transition can be traced to the church coming to a knowledge of who it is and what it must be about. We are on mission for our Lord.

IV
Rural-Urban Fringe Churches

16.
First Baptist Church
Taylorsville, Kentucky
Harold S. Mauney, Pastor

The author of this case study was born in Corbin, Kentucky. He is a graduate of Georgetown College in his home state and also the Southern Baptist Theological Seminary where he was awarded the Master of Divinity degree. Mauney has served as the pastor of four churches in Tennessee and Kentucky. He and his wife, Donna, are the parents of a daughter. He enjoys golfing and fishing.

The First Baptist Church, Taylorsville, Kentucky, is about to be involved in a dramatic transition. The changes in the community served by the church are resulting from the construction of a reservoir by the U.S. Army Corps of Engineers, and the construction of a highway by the Kentucky Department of Highways. The new highway will put rural Taylorsville within a few minutes drive of Louisville, the largest city in Kentucky.

Our preparation for the transition is not complete, but we are beginning. This study will show where the church is at a certain point in the process.

The First Baptist Church is in the county seat town of Spencer County. It is a Southern Baptist congregation. The population of Taylorsville is one thousand. However, in the immediate area live about twenty-five hundred additional people. Since 1950 the county population has been on the decline, from 6,157 to 5,488. The town population has remained stable.

Spencer County is adjacent to Jefferson County and metro Louisville. The bulk of the work force in Spencer is employed in Jefferson County. While other counties surrounding Jefferson have grown over the past twenty years, Spencer has not. This has been due to poor roads and lack of available land. The construction of the reservoir is changing both these factors.

We celebrated our 150th anniversary during July 1978. Rev. William Stout, a pioneer Baptist preacher from Virginia, was the first pastor. His ministry spanned the early years of the church. The first building was constructed in 1830. It is still standing today and is used as a residence.

In 1854 a new building on a new location was planned. It was dedicated in 1858 under the leadership of Rev. Joseph Weaver. In addition to the price of the lot, the new building cost $5,000, a tremendous effort for a congregation of 182 members. During that same year, a community Sabbath School was organized in Taylorsville. It first met in the Baptist church. Consequently, the group became a part of the work of the church.

In 1864, during the hardships of the War Between the States, the final mortgage was paid. In 1868 the church joined with other members of the Long Run Baptist Association for a regular collection for missions.

The present church building was dedicated July 11, 1915. Extensive renovation and redecoration were done to the sanctuary in 1968, making the church a beautiful example of turn of the century decor.

Under the dynamic leadership of Dr. A. Mack Parrish, the church constructed an educational building in 1925. This building is still in use but has undergone interior remodeling.

Since 1968 the church has purchased three houses and lots. Two of the old houses have been torn down and the lots are used for parking and recreation. One of the houses is used for rental property.

The church has a rich history. It has been a stable influence through the years. Its history has been marked by dedicated men, women and young people who have been faithful servants of the Lord.

The table on the opposite page summarizes the church's ministry during the past year.

We now have an active day camp, backyard Bible clubs, and youth retreats. There are outreach and evangelism activities that include traditional revivals and visitation emphasis. The church sponsors a rebroadcast of our regular morning worship service over a local radio station.

Organization	Enrollment
Sunday School	263
Music Ministry	71
Woman's Missionary Union	75
Royal Ambassadors	26
Vacation Bible School	110
Total gifts to all causes	$68,610
Total gifts to missions	7,023
Additions by baptism	10
Additions by letter	16
Total resident members	583
Net membership gain for year	10

Over the past ten years, in a declining to stable population, the church has received an average of twenty-one new members per year. The most significant growth has been in finances. Since 1969 gifts have increased by 61 percent.

A look at the present ministry indicates a typical small county seat town church ministering to its community through traditional Baptist programs. However, the church will not be able to stay a quiet little church in a quiet little town. All of that is about to change. The construction of the reservoir will significantly increase population in Spencer County and the area served by First Baptist Church.

On November 7, 1966 the Eighty-Ninth Congress authorized Section 203 of Public Law 89-789. This action set in motion plans by the Corps of Engineers to construct the Taylorsville Reservoir. This project is for the purposes of flood control in the Salt River Basin, general recreation, fish and wildlife sporting, water conservation, and water quality control.

The proposed dam is three and one-half miles southwest of the town. When flooded, the lake will cover more than three thousand acres across three counties. More than 70 percent of the water coverage will be in Spencer. It is expected to be completed by 1982.

Adjacent to the reservoir and lake, the Kentucky Department

of Parks and Recreation proposes construction of a 2,000 acre park for recreation and camping. All of the park will be in Spencer County. The main entrance will be five miles from town.

Concurrent with the completion of the reservoir, the Kentucky Department of Highways plans a road from the dam site into Jefferson County. This road will pass close to Taylorsville with a connector into town. When the highway is completed next year, Spencer County will be within a few miles of the Louisville area.

Significant population changes are forecast to occur in Spencer County upon completion of these projects. This table gives a summary:

Date	Spencer Co. Population	Percent
1950	6,157	
1960	5,680	−7.7
1970	5,488	−3.4
1980	6,235	+14.0
1990	7,523	+21.0
2000	9,781	+30.0

From these estimates it can be noted the population in Spencer County has "bottomed out" and will be starting up during the coming years.

"Second home" population increase includes weekend visitors and vacationers with recreation homes in the lake area. Also, permanent homes will be built and significant increases are projected for both the elementary and secondary schools.

The reservoir is destined to bring a large number of visitors to the lake. The estimate by the Corps is in excess of one million! The proximity of Jefferson County accounts for this large estimate.

The spectacular growth of Spencer County will cause an obvious adjustment in our rural thought patterns. With the coming of new people from more urbanized areas, adjustments must be made at every institutional level: county government, the school system, businesses, and the churches.

Taylorsville First Baptist is a church about to be caught up in transition. The church is a stable, small town church. There will be a need for significant planning for the church to meet these challenges.

In helping the church prepare for the changes I developed an extensive questionnaire and pre-tested it in a small group. After some modification, the questionnaire was given to Sunday school classes and the deacons.

The questionnaire was to measure the attitude of the people toward the changes that are ahead.

The results would give us an idea of the direction to take in preparing the church to cope with the changes.

Of the one hundred questionnaries distributed, fifty-eight were returned. There was an even distribution by age group response. The questionnaire was divided into two sections dealing with the future of the community and the future of the church.

The results of the questionnaire were very positive: 76 percent said they felt the church had a definite idea of what God wanted it to be and do. The same percent listed evangelism and outreach as the most important task of the church. Forty-five percent indicated outreach would continue to be the single most important objective over the next seven to ten years, and 86 percent felt the church had adequate talent and resources to accomplish its desired goals.

The majority of the respondents foresaw a changing community imposed by reservoir construction; 45 percent indicated the community would become a resort-recreational community while twenty-six percent saw a suburban-residential community. When the reservoir is completed, 72 percent saw a significant population increase while 50 percent said the reservoir will help the community.

According to 76 percent of the respondents, social problems will increase in the county during the next seven to ten years.

Basic concerns for the church were listed as: reaching the spiritually unsaved, contacting people moving into the community, establishing a resort ministry in the park, and working with juvenile delinquents.

The present programs of the church will not be adequate according to 41 percent of those returning the questionnaire. The youth ministry will need to be strengthened the most. The size of the present church staff is not adequate for the next several years, so said 43 percent and 60 percent indicated a need for a full time minister of music and youth.

Fifty-two percent said the facilities are not adequate for the future, and 83 percent said the greatest need would be a recreational facility.

There will be a few problems accepting and assimilating new people as they join the church fellowship. This statement received a 79 percent approval. A sizable number, 64 percent, said the church would be flexible enough to meet the challenge of a changing community.

The overall response was positive. Most seemed to be aware of the challenge facing the church. Opinion is divided on what type of community the area will become, but we recognize that the community will not remain as it is.

The questionnaire made the congregation realize the need for serious thinking about change. It was a meaningful first step in preparation for transition.

I have studied seriously five churches who found themselves in similar circumstances to ours. My research included questions about the status of the churches before and after reservoir construction, long-range planning before completion of the reservoir, resort ministries, and assimilation of new people.

None of the churches surveyed engaged in long-range planning prior to reservoir construction. None of these churches reported significant growth even though there was a population increase. This has led me to conclude that there seems to be real correlation between growth and planning for growth.

An aggressive resort ministry does not mean increased statistical growth within the church. The resort ministry must be viewed as the church giving of itself in ministry. A resort ministry must be well planned and executed to be effective.

A changing community does not guarantee an aggressive, outreach-minded church. A church can easily be just what it was before.

A church can be in the midst of a fast growing area and still be an "island unto itself" if it is not committed to the mission of Jesus Christ.

This study had a sobering effect on the people of our church. It helped all of us realize that church growth is not automatic. It also helped us to see the need for effective planning.

With the appointment of a long-range planning committee in the spring of 1976, the church began to think seriously about its future.

The committee studied the present church program strengths and weaknesses and noted areas of needed improvement. The committee sought all available sources for impact the reservoir would make on the community. When this was completed, the committee faced the task of interpretation to the church. The results of the questionnaire made this easier.

The committee's work continues. High on the priority list is a definite resort ministry and an increased program for children and youth.

The committee is using the manual, *Leading Your Church In Long Range Planning*, by Reginald M. McDonough (Nashville: Convention Press, 1975). This has been an invaluable guide to both pastor and committee members.

The long-range planning committee was elected for an indefinite period. This group plans to continue as a follow-up committee to guide the church in implementing its plans. This will give some continuity between what is planned and what is accomplished. As the commitee continues its work over the next few months, new opportunities will be discovered and plans for ministry will be made.

The church has received well the efforts to plan for the future. There have been no major obstacles to overcome so far. The most difficult part will be to implement the plans as the needs arise. Every precaution will be taken to see that this is done.

Our members are aware that change is coming. There seems to be a "what do we do now?" attitude on the part of our leaders. Only the future will tell the reaction to specific plans and needs as we face a dynamic rapid community transition.

17.
Paw Creek Presbyterian Church
Paw Creek, North Carolina
Jefferson K. Aiken Jr., Pastor

Jeff Aiken is a native of Baton Rouge, Louisiana. He received the Bachelor of Science Degree from Louisiana State University, the Master of Divinity Degree from Columbia Theological Seminary, Decatur, Georgia, and the Doctor of Ministry Degree from McCormick Theological Seminary, Chicago. Prior to entering the ministry, he worked as a television news anchorman. He currently serves as a church goal-setting consultant and has a weekly feature on a Charlotte, North Carolina, television station. Aiken became pastor of Paw Creek Church in 1973.

Paw Creek Presbyterian Church, organized and chartered in 1809, is one of the oldest congregations in Mecklenburg Presbytery. Near the church is a small stream, named Paw Creek by the Indians because of the large number of Papaw trees growing upon its banks. From this creek the church took its name.

For nearly 150 years the rural one-building church had been attended and supported primarily by a half-dozen families and their descendents who lived in the Paw Creek area.

Then during the late 1950s the area surrounding the church began growing and changing. Business, industry, and housing developments began appearing on what was formerly forest and farmland. The church made a gradual and positive transition from a rural church of a few families to a suburban church of 550 members with many new families.

While early pastoral leadership played a great role in the growth, a survey of the church members we retained pointed out that very few persons joined the church because of a particular minister or because the minister visited their home. Most people answered that they joined Paw Creek because a friend invited them, or because the people in the congregation were friendly.

Many older members reflect upon this in a fashion similar to Adrian Cathey, a 75-year old elder emeritus, who has held various leadership positions in the church since his youth. Cathey states, "I feel that the change in our church over the last twenty years has been basically due to the openness with which our people have expressed their friendliness to those who have moved into our community. They have been sincerely welcomed by the members and at the same time oriented into the program of the church. I think this did a lot to bring about a unity of fellowship which still carries forth today."

Margie Campbell, one of the church's senior members, notes that a high trust level was nurtured as "the new members did not push themselves into leadership. Older members, seeing the capabilities of the newcomers, gradually began working them into leadership positions within the church."

Paw Creek Presbyterian Church is in Mecklenburg County, seven miles northwest of downtown Charlotte, North Carolina. The area has no single, major employer, although more trucking lines are headquartered here than in any other southern city. Mecklenburg Presbytery has more Presbyterians per square mile than any other presbytery in the Presbyterian Church U.S. Five Presbyterian churches and about twenty-five other denominations are within a four mile radius of our church. Paw Creek has throughout its history given generously of its members to begin these neighboring Presbyterian churches, most recently in 1967 when 139 members formed Memorial Presbyterian Church, three miles away.

The church property is close to an industrial area. Within a quarter mile are oil terminals and storage tanks for many of the major oil companies. Adjacent to the church is a former high school which has been used in recent years by the Board of Education for storage.

While much of the property near Paw Creek is rather unattractive, the church buildings and grounds are beautiful and well kept. Situated in a grove of oak trees, the buildings consist of a sanctuary with educational wings on both sides and a fellowship building in the rear. Behind this is the church cemetery.

The sanctuary, which seats four hundred, was erected in 1882 and has been remodeled and refurnished a number of times. These facilities are all well maintained and adequate for Paw Creek's congregation.

Beyond the industrial perimeter, which extends only a half mile in a semi-circle near the church, are numerous residential areas. Most of these are white communities of middle class and upper middle class status. There is a small black community about two and a half miles from the church.

Age and economic status of the surrounding communities vary considerably. First there is the Thrift Road Community, an older, settled area. Newer suburban residential communities have developed nearby within the past twenty years. Most of these communities are middle and upper middle class.

The Thrift Road community, from which most of the church's older members and about 35 percent of the church's total population comes, is south of a nearby railroad track. The homes are on or near Thrift Road, a main artery leading into the city. Most of the houses are modest wooden frame or brick homes. The majority of the members living in this area are more than fifty years old, have been members of Paw Creek since birth, and are, or have been, church officers. While few of these persons are college educated, most have good jobs or have retired from good jobs. While not affluent, most would be considered middle class.

Approximately a mile and a half due north of the church is another residential area known as Coulwood Hills. In fourteen years this section has gradually grown to more than seven hundred homes. The current market value of these residences ranges from $35,000 to $125,000. Most of those in the community are well established executive or professional people under fifty years old who are not generally subject to job transfers. The majority of them are college educated.

The church has experienced a steady flow of new members from this area. Half of the church members reside here, and many of the community leaders also hold positions of leadership in the church.

About 15 percent of the members come from surrounding areas

other than the two mentioned. These other communities would be considered middle class and upper middle class. None of these areas is highly transient, enabling the church to enjoy a certain amount of stability while allowing it to maintain a rather orderly growth pattern.

One of the hallmarks of the church is that it is a congregation of unity with diversity. The members take pride in the fact that there has never been a church split. Members have sometimes left to form or be a part of new congregations, but always departing under pleasant circumstances. Church members frequently hold opposing opinions; however, they are able to deal with their differences in a mature manner and with respect for their differences.

New members are often given leadership positions within a relatively short time. The session and board of deacons (fifteen members each) operate on a rotating basis with members serving three year terms as elected by the congregation. The average age of the board of deacons is thirty-eight, with only three members over forty-five years old. On the session, the average age is about fifty-three, with ten members over forty-five years of age.

All of the current officers are men. Women have been nominated for office several times, but they have never been elected by the congregation, although many observers predict that women soon will be.

There is a high level of trust between the session and the board of deacons. Both use highly discretionary powers in their areas of jurisdiction, with the diaconate giving primary leadership in finances, and the session in programs. Although these bodies meet together infrequently, few communication mishaps seem to occur. Only once in the past 15 years has the session vetoed an action of the diaconate, which in the Presbyterian system is subservient to the session.

Contributions have risen and kept abreast of inflation. While many members have excellent jobs and good incomes, it should be noted that there are no extremely wealthy persons on the church rolls. Benevolent giving, which has been comparatively low in the past, tripled between 1973-1977.

As benevolent giving increased, so did the church's sense of mis-

Table of Members * and Contributions

Year	Active Members	Benevolences	Expenses	Total Contributions
1930	339	1,748	3,710	6,277
1940	297	954	2,583	3,570
1950	393	4,763	8,445	13,208
1960	435	7,381	35,518	51,026
1970	511	11,292	56,891	86,888
1977	527	31,283	88,600	139,633

* Many Presbyterian churches have a practice of reviewing their rolls every year, placing those who have shown no participation on an inactive roll. Paw Creek adheres to this practice and the membership figures reflect only the active roll.

sion in the community. In recent years the church has used its buildings for a weekday kindergarten program, homemakers' extension clubs, and community civic organizations.

A social services fund was established ten years ago through the estate of a deceased member. Church members have subsequently contributed generously to the fund. Its purpose is to provide money for persons in the community of the church whose circumstances may warrant such help. A committee of three, along with the pastor, decides on these gifts, with information on the recipients kept in confidence. Gifts in the $400-$600 range are not uncommon.

The church has a strong interest in world missions, supporting a missionary family in Haiti. In addition, the congregation recently gave $23,000 to a Presbytery project in Haiti to help alleviate hunger. Last fall two men from the congregation gave three weeks of their time to work on the Haitian project.

The women of the church, individually and collectively, have served as Red Cross Volunteers at Presbyterian Hospital, provided occasional senior citizens luncheons, and worked with day care centers and church Bible Schools in a black community.

About forty-five junior and senior high youths participate in the church's youth program.

Many activities help create fellowship: an annual Thanksgiving breakfast, an annual dinner on the grounds, several family night suppers, an annual weekend church retreat attended by more than two hundred persons, many large church school parties, low cost dinners every evening during the family Vacation Church School.

The congregation is closely bound together through kinship and fellowship. Even with the influx of new members during recent years, the church continues to have an unusually large number of members who are relatives. This has not been a problem in the church since there is no one dominant family or faction. After Sunday morning worship, people frequently stand around fifteen to thirty minutes conversing with one another. This behavior has produced depth relationships among many members and has helped newer members to become readily accepted into the congregation.

Glenn Cathey, who became the church treasurer in the late 1950s now tells with a grin on his face how the church's only financial records were turned over to him in a dog-eared spiral notebook. According to all indications, this was typical of the haphazard ways in which most matters were administered at Paw Creek until the 1960s. The question has often been raised: "How did Paw Creek make the transition from a lethargic rural congregation to an active, efficiently administered, multi-staff suburban congregation?"

In a recent survey one hundred random members answered a questionnaire giving their reasons. When provided with a list of suggestions relative to the positive transition, most persons who were church members at that time rated pastoral leadership at the top of the list.

About 1957, during the pastorate of an elderly minister nearing retirement, the church attendance and membership began declining. Those who were members then recall the low morale. Upon the retirement of the older minister in 1958, another minister was called.

The new minister, Edward Craig, was thirty-two years old, with much enthusiasm about the possibilities for the church. Coulwood Hills was just beginning to develop near the church and during Craig's ministry many new members were received from this area. The pastor operated philosophically from the stance of an evangelical minister with a good sense of organization. His preaching contained more theological depth than the average pastor's and he was apparently able to relate his theological content in a meaningful way to the congregation. During Craig's eight-year pastorate, a secretary was employed, a director of Christian education was called, a new wing was added to the church, a new manse was built, and a weekday kindergarten was begun. The church increased in membership from 357 to 634 during this time.

About four months after Craig's departure in 1966, another minister, Robert J. James, was called. James' style of ministry was somewhat different from Craig's. James was a business executive before entering the ministry. He had the appearance and bearing of a top corporate executive, plus the warmth of a good minister. Persons in the church seemed to develop rapid confidence in his ability.

Being a first-class organizer and administrator, he continued to build on the organizational structure which was begun by Craig. James improved the administrative aspect of the church's program as he and the clerk of session organized an outstanding church manual. The manual, which is updated from time to time, is given to each church officer, and continues to be a most effective tool in the understanding of church policy. During his pastorate a new educational wing with modern church offices was built at a cost of $150,000. Today the church has net assets at slightly under one million dollars.

Robert James left Paw Creek in 1973 to become general presbyter (chief executive officer) of Mecklenburg Presbytery. By the time of his departure, the church had made a smooth transition to a suburban congregation.

Besides good pastoral leadership and a genuine openness to the community, the smooth transition happened because of the organizational development of the church. Before 1960, the church had operated with permanent church officers. A person was elected to serve the church as an elder or deacon for life, and seldom were changes made in the session or diaconate, except as someone died or moved.

Shortly after Craig became the church's pastor, he suggested that the church change to the rotation (or limited term of service) system for the session and diaconate. Adrian Cathey again says, "About this time we had several members of the session who were sixty to seventy-five years old. As you know, many times men of this age don't go along with many new ideas and changes, but only one man seemed to oppose the new ideas suggested by the new minister."

As joint responsibilities were assumed by the new members, working in partnership with older members, a majority of the congregation began feeling ownership in the old church which was being revitalized. Under new leaders and new directions, the trust level continued an upward momentum as the congregation demonstrated a receptiveness to change.

However, while many of the structural and administrative shortcomings of the congregation were laid to rest, Paw Creek did not do away with all of its past. The church is still very traditional in many respects, although, through its officers, the congregation does seem to dispense with the customs of the past which tend to be counterproductive. This could be summed up by a line from the church's statement of purpose which says it is the intent of the church "To by loyal to the best of the past, open to new understandings of the truth, and pioneering new paths of worship, learnings, and service."

The ability to look forward and backward at the same time allows the church to realize its historical strengths as well as its potential.

During the past five years the church has been involved in several goal setting processes. These events, some of which have involved the entire congregation, have been well received by the members. Each year the church committees have definite goals which are adopted and finalized by the session. Included among the current goals are plans for a new multi-purpose building and gymanasium.

Robert Worley, of McCormick Seminary, has pointed out that "goalless congregations tend to select goalless leaders." [4] Paw Creek was once one of those goalless organizations until the late 1950s and early 1960s when it began selecting ministers and officers who were more inclined to be goal oriented.

In goal setting, the minister assumes the role of equipping the members. He becomes the one who helps others to help themselves discover their special gifts.

As Worley has stated, "To recognize the church as the body of Christ places a mandate before churchmen to become persons committed to the role of agents of change for the institutional church. They will dare to struggle with new or transformed structures for caring for the church and the world. They will seek new or transformed processes for communication, decision-making, and interaction through which the gifts of all members can be received, appreciated, and shared both within the church and without. Most important, they will be agents who will try to discover appropriate theological expressions to support and maintain the life of the body of Christ in ministry and mission." [5]

Of course, the change in the style and the image of Paw Creek would have never transpired without the surrounding community. The influx of new people—dedicated, gifted and capable, working with the older members who possessed deep spiritual roots, kindness, and affection for their new neighbors—served to comprise a harmonious and compatible relationship for the future.

18.
First Israel Baptist Church
Belle Alliance, Louisiana
Alvin C. Daniels, Pastor

This case study was written by the Rev. Alvin C. Daniels who was born in Donaldsonville, Louisiana. He received his Bachelor of Arts degree from Leland College in Baker, Louisiana. Later he taught social science, physical education, coached, and was Assistant Principal at Lowery High School in his hometown. Daniels graduated also from the New Orleans Baptist Theological Seminary and did further study at New York University. He is the pastor of Philippian Baptist Church at Union, Louisiana, in addition to being the pastor of First Israel.

The small unincorporated community of Belle Alliance in Assumption Parish is situated seventy miles west of New Orleans and forty-five miles east of Baton Rouge. In the middle of the sugar cane belt, it is home for about thirty-five hundred residents.

Over the years, the people have earned their living in the fields. Twenty years ago a pronounced change began to occur in the area when oil refineries started to spring up across the rural landscape. Many people left the sugar cane farms and went to work in the refineries on the banks of the Mississippi River.

Since then, new people have come to work in the refineries and they have built houses in the vicinity. Also, more and more individuals who have lived and worked in and around Belle Alliance all their lives are now driving to New Orleans and Baton Rouge for employment. At the same time, families from those two growing cities are moving closer to Belle Alliance each week. Our rural community is changing.

While personal income and fringe benefits have improved in recent years, other problems have arisen. The need for child-care during working hours has become apparent. Tension in the schools has risen and the use of drugs among the youth has occurred. Some barriers have been created between the new-comers and the old-timers. We are no longer just a rural community; we are becoming more urban all the time.

The First Israel Baptist Church was organized as a black congregation in 1865. A preacher from New Orleans, the Rev. Joseph P. Davenport, organized the church and was the pastor for nearly twenty years. He pulled together a membership of 160 people. A total of six pastors, including myself, have served the church.

Across the years the pastors have given careful attention to education. Before blacks could attend public schools and universities, the church sponsored Israel Academy for community residents, and assisted in supporting the Houma Academy. Years ago the church operated a benevolent society for people in distress and a funeral home for our members.

I became the pastor of First Israel in 1950. At the time we had 143 members. As a church we try to serve people from the cradle to the grave. I have sought to instill in our laity a vision of what the church should be doing in caring for others. It is my conviction that a church will proceed in Christian ministry only as far as the pastor leads them and that the work of the church starts with individuals where they are. We have made some steps to meet needs in our changing community and we are making plans for the wave of the future.

Prior to discussing our hopes and plans for tomorrow, let me mention what we have been doing. Before bus transportation was available for school children, we provided a bus. It helped also in transporting both children and adults to church services on Sunday.

Before public schools had kindergartens, one was held for twenty-three years in our building. It has since been developed into a day-care center for the children of working parents. Our center has been used on a number of occasions as a place of protective care for children whose lives were in danger at home.

As more and more mothers went to work in the 1960s a critical need arose for the washing and cleaning of clothes for families. Due to segregation laws no washateria was available in our area for blacks. Consequently, we formed a separate corporation from

the church to build a community washateria. In order to finance
the project, individual members of the church bought in the washateria, and the church voted to purchase stock. This venture met
a great need and continues to do so even though the segregation
laws have disappeared.

Houses in the area were far less than desirable for decades. Realizing that the life of the pastor often becomes an example for others
in the black community, a decision was made to build a nice parsonage. Within a short time remodeled homes began to appear
and new houses were erected. On another occasion one of our members on limited income was living in a shack. Our congregation
made a decision to buy a house for the member. It was understood
that the church would have no equity in the property because all
we wanted to do was meet a personal need.

In the last several years, we have acquired some equipment for
the care of the sick in our community. On a regular basis we loan
(free of charge) a hospital bed, walker, and wheelchair.

We have had much success in working with teenagers and young
adults. Each May, a well-planned youth retreat is held for spiritual,
emotional, and social enrichment. In addition a career day is on
our annual schedule to help young people discover their gifts and
plan for the future. Physicians, teachers, farmers, clergymen,
mechanics, lawyers, nurses, and other individuals from many walks
of life lead the discussions each year and answer questions.

Our position on race always has been one of an open door policy.
We are at home with any Christian in our midst, regardless of
color. At least twice every year we have white ministers preach in
our services of worship, lead revivals, or teach study courses. Twenty-
eight years ago our Sunday offerings averaged about $30.00 per
week. Our financial support system was for each member to give
twenty-five cents per month, and nearly everyone stayed two months
behind in their giving. As a church we were at a standstill. My
wife and I tithed our income weekly, not only to fulfill biblical
instruction and help the church, but to be an example for the membership. It took three years before the people began to realize what
could be done if we tithed. A remarkable change has occurred in

every aspect of our work since then, especially in facility construction, evangelism, and missions.

Our main building was finished in 1960. It serves as our central place for worship but also includes classrooms, a kitchen, and offices. In 1973 we converted a former school house into our day care center. I now own my own home and the church parsonage has been transformed into a fellowship hall.

A consistent emphasis has been devoted to evangelistic efforts. All of our organizations have evangelism at the center of their activities. The Women's Missionary Union, the Brotherhood, the Sunday School, and Vacation Bible School serve to make persons aware of salvation through Jesus Christ. Our Training Union is active in providing instruction for new and growing Christians. Revivals are held each year and regular visits to spiritually lost people are conducted week after week. Our membership now has reached four hundred.

The worship services each Sunday are well planned but are not formal and stiff. We leave plenty of room for individual expression. Through our worship we seek to give purpose and meaning to life; to remind everyone of our ultimate dependency on God; to find some answers to life's problems; and to receive personal salvation. At the worship hour we always extend a sincere invitation to anyone to respond to God's love through Christ.

A missionary spirit has been created which has been a real blessing to the church family. We have four mission circles at work in four distinct areas of our larger community. We have invited local, state, national, and international speakers to enlarge our awareness of missions. In 1975, we responded to an emergency plea from the Foreign Mission Board of our National Baptist Convention, U.S.A., Inc., and sent $1,000 to a hospital in Africa. We have also "adopted" a child in Africa who needs an education.

A carefully planned church program includes immediate and long-range goals and objectives which are means to an end and not ends in themselves. As First Israel plans for the future, we are keeping in mind the following factors which we view as essential: worship, evangelism, religious education, financial stewardship, adequate buildings, community service, and missions.

In particular, we are establishing plans for the construction of a modern educational unit. We want it to house a comprehensive library for the students from our community who commute thirty-five miles to Nicholls State University at Thibodaux, Louisiana, and to Southern University at Baton Rouge. We know that a library in the students' home community will assist them immeasurably with their research and studies. We have young people in our church and in the area who travel by bus to the universities each day and, as a result, have limited access to a library.

We are seeing an increasing number of senior adults in our community. Hence, we are developing a council on aging in the church with the possibility of creating a day care center for older citizens.

Recently a point of tension has arisen among some of our members over the use of government funds. Some of our younger members want us to use government money for our projects but other members do not. Over the years the congregation has been trained to support itself and stand on our own feet. We are resolving these delicate feelings as carefully as possible in the spirit of Christ our Lord.

As Belle Alliance moves from being strictly a rural community to a rural-urban area, it is obvious that hard work is in store for us as a church. More training seminars in church development and community ministries will be needed. The talents and abilities of our people must be drawn out and enhanced on a greater scale than in the past. We could use the services of seminary interns to help us in our development, especially with educational, music and youth needs and opportunities.

In light of the past, we welcome the challenges of the present and of the future to be faithful to our Savior. We are trusting him to lead us as he knows best.

19.
First Baptist Church
Concord, Tennessee
Joe R. Stacker, Pastor

Joe Stacker is a native of Greenbrier, Tennessee. He received his formal education at Carson-Newman College and the Southern Baptist Theological Seminary where he was awarded the Master of Divinity and Doctor of Ministry degrees. He and his wife, Anna Lee, are the parents of two daughters. He has served as the pastor of four churches.

The village of Concord is an unincorporated settlement located on the banks of the Tennessee River in the east-central section of the state. It is fifteen miles west of Knoxville and twelve miles southeast of Oak Ridge.

For many years the area was fertile farm country that supplied Knoxville with fresh vegetables, milk, and beef. In 1875 it was a good-half day trip by wagon to Knoxville. Change came slowly in those days.

In 1890 a marble deposit was discovered on the banks of the Tennessee River and quarriers from Virginia moved in to work the mine. Several members of the group were Southern Baptists. Finding no Baptist church in Concord, they proceeded to organize one. From 1890s until 1933 the development of the church was slow but steady. Student pastors from Carson-Newman College, a Southern Baptist school in near-by Jefferson City, would come by train on the second and fourth Sundays to conduct worship services.

In 1928 Concord Baptist Church felt the need for a new location and moved two blocks down the street. A new name was given to the church—Crichton Memorial—in memory of Crichton Bevins whose family gave the money for the new sanctuary.

The 1930s saw major change arrive in the mountains of East Tennessee when the federal government organized the Tennessee

Valley Authority. This was an all-out effort to provide flood control and inexpensive electricity to one of the most impoverished areas of the nation. Soon provincialism was disturbed, especially in 1943 when the scientific community of Oak Ridge was instituted by the Atomic Energy Commission. It was a multibillion dollar project offering jobs by the thousands. Immediately new families came into the surrounding area, and a host of them bought or built houses in Concord. The quaint ways of the hills started to give way to "citified" manners. The pace of life would never be the same again as tourism developed rapidly.

Acute transition hit Concord in 1945 when the Fort Loudon Dam was built. Soon one-half of the town's acreage was covered by water and many families were up-rooted and relocated. The traditional, quiet community was broken up indeed.

The numerical growth of the church continued through the 1940s and an educational complex was added. In the early 1950s the first full-time pastor was called. This began an unprecedented period of outreach and development for the church. More space was needed for parking as well as for Sunday School and worship services. Plans began to emerge for relocation in keeping with the growth boom taking place in the entire area. The farms were becoming subdivisions. The once quite countryside became filled with children, cars, houses, and fast-food stores. The move of the church to a highly visible place would mean unlimited growth.

Crichton Memorial moved to its present site on Kingston Pike in 1962. This is a four-lane federal highway which thousands of people travel each day. At the time of the move the name of the congregation was changed to First Baptist Church of Concord.

The growth and development of First Baptist since 1962 has been extraordinary. When the church moved, there were 320 members. Six years later the number had increased to 650 and today it has reached 2,100. Over one thousand people have been baptized into the church since 1962.

In the main, the program and ministry of the church has been structured with two basic criteria in mind, namely, demand and planning. The demand criteria was obvious, i.e. a growing community demanded a growing church. The planning criteria recognized that in order to meet the needs of a booming community the development of strategic plans by the church would be essential.

Our approach has been built around the use of long-range planning materials produced by the Sunday School Board of the Southern Baptist Convention. We established a functioning church council composed of the organizational leaders. We made committee work a vital part of our ongoing planning strategy.

The use of the laypersons as church officers gives more congregational participation to the planning groups. The church's staff of ministers acts in a leadership role along with all elected church leaders.

Planning at First Baptist Church has involved the Knox County Metropolitan Planning Commission and has taken into account public school growth and local community surveys. *The Church Commitment Planning Guide* by Truman Brown Jr. has proven an invaluable aid in completing the task of yearly planning. We plan by phases. For instance our last planning effort was for 1976-80. Included in that study were concerns such as: (1) community growth; (2) church staff needs; (3) missions and evangelism; (4) worship—music development; (5) Christian education; (6) properties and equipment; (7) youth ministry; (8) special ministries; (9) stewardship—time and money; (10) motivation in a Baptist church; and (11) food services.

The planning for church growth and ministry demanded a look at the people. More than 50 percent of First Baptist Church's people have a college education. Many have advanced degrees. This placed a strong emphasis on quality programs and top-notch Bible teaching.

The growth of the church called for attention to new members. A new member's class has been ongoing for the past eight years, using materials written by the Church Administration Department of the Sunday School Board as well as some special materials developed by our church. These classes meet for five weeks on Sunday evenings during the Church Training Program. The importance of this class is evident when one realizes that every five years First Baptist Church has a thirty-five percent turnover. At least fifty percent of our members were not reared in East Tennessee.

To cope with growth, two morning worship services each week were conducted from 1969 until 1973. The construction of a twelve hundred seat sanctuary led the church to two Sunday Schools with one worship service. Since 1975, this has given opportunity for continued growth without the cost of new facilities.

The two Sunday Schools were beneficial until 1978 when the program became an apparent burden to those who worked in the late Sunday School. Inability to recruit workers led the church to adopt an alternating plan with Sunday School at 9:15 A.M. for all but the youth division which was in worship. At 10:30 A.M. the youth attend Sunday School while the morning worship service is held.

The one Sunday School organization gave opportunity to increase the units in the adult division and helped the church to move toward a new educational building program. The organization for the new building was already set before the building was finished.

Challenging people to ministry and witness is accomplished in several ways. Weekly visitation is promoted in all the organizations with Sunday School being the primary focal group. Special church-wide events such as revivals, visitation suppers, music programs, family life conferences, Bible studies, media presentations, and selected guest speakers are used to aid in making people aware of their Christian commitment.

In a church such as ours communication has been a challenge. The people are scattered over an area twenty miles long and six miles wide. A weekly newsletter is mailed to all members and visitors. Advertisements are placed in the local newspapers with good use made of the local radio free "bulletin board" announcements. Consideration is being given to television programming of Sunday services. To help tell the story of First Baptist, an annual newspaper is mailed each fall to nine thousand residents in our area.

To aid in the many contacts made to our members, a computer service was set up in 1978. Maintaining contact with two thousand individuals or 650 family units demands a great deal of secretarial work, but the computer has enabled the church to make more than three hundred thousand different contacts each year at one-third the cost of an additional secretary. This program has aided in the ministry concerns of the church. Keeping up with a transient people is difficult at best. Yet this is a must if fellowship is to be maintained and developed.

In ministry we maintain these programs: (1) homebound department; (2) keenagers (senior adult club); (3) deacon family ministry plan; (4) weekday early education; (5) services at a rescue mission and a health care center; (6) Scout programs; and (7) community organizational use of our buildings.

To encourage ministry in the church the 1978-79 planning was done around the theme, "Fellowship in the Family of God." As a part of this emphasis the church held four "Family Weeks at Home." During these weeks families were encouraged to do things together, invite other church families into their homes who had not previously visited there, and to share a word of love and appreciation to someone in the church.

Theme planning has some great possibilities for church growth and development. Some past themes used at First Baptist are "A Great Commission Church"; "Where Do We Go From Here?"; and "A Year of Prayer."

To expand the horizons of the congregation an overall missions involvement has been carried on for the past seven years. The work of foreign missions is encouraged through the traditional programs in the church. A plus for us is the service of Bob and Ronnie Erwin in Brazil. The Erwins are from our congregation. A highlight of this effort came in 1977 when three men from our church went to Brazil on a working mission tour. This vision has led to a growing awareness and commitment to missions in other places.

At home First Baptist sponsors the work of the University Baptist Church in Brookings, South Dakota. Financial assistance is sent each month, and we go on mission tours to the area at least every two years. More than 150 members of the church have been to Brookings in the past five years. We have come to realize that without a vision the people perish.

To undergird the ministry of a changing church there must be money. In 1968 the budget of the church was $90,000. In 1978 the budget was $490,000. To aid in the stewardship of money we have used several approaches. A direct mail effort was quite good. The most successful program came with the use of the Southern Baptist Convention Stewardship Commission materials entitled "Tither Commitment Program." The year-round tithing emphasis has been followed for several years. Special building funds were established in the past and will continue as long as the church has to build new facilities.

In 1978 the church began use of the monthly envelope service of the Baptist Sunday School Board. This gives each church member a monthly reminder of his or her stewardship responsibilities.

Budget development has changed with the growth of the church. A practice begun in 1976 was to budget according to ministry needs. If an organization could not justify in ministry the dollars requested, the amount was lowered or eliminated. Ministry-oriented budget planning enabled our leaders to look more carefully at what we were seeking to do as a New Testament church.

Along with the budget goals, a system of money controls was set up to give a clear picture of who was spending the money budgeted. An annual audit is made of the financial records and reported to the church through the stewardship committee.

A growing church calls for increased staff members. In 1968 there were three paid employees of the church: pastor, secretary, and custodian. At present, the staff numbers twenty-eight people who receive a payroll check from the church. There are five ministers, four secretaries, a church hostess, a cook, two custodians, and fifteen teachers and aides.

The pastor and other ministers see themselves as player/coaches seeking to share Christ with people in a changing community. Weekly staff meetings are held where the schedule and program for the next week are discussed. This is the continuation of a staff retreat held in the late spring by the five ministers.

Not all that has happened has been readily accepted by the church. There are times when people have reacted to change in the community. Many citizens strongly resented the post office being made a branch of Knoxville. Concord is where people live and they are proud of their local identity. Growth has caused some of our members to seek smaller churches. As Lyle Schaller notes it, we have experienced the conflict between the "homesteaders and the pioneers." Some people left the church because for them it was becoming too large. Others have left because of their disregard for the "professional" ways of the staff as well as for modern budget procedures. Last year sixty-six individuals departed to start a new church in our growing area. This growth situation will, according to the Knox County Metropolitan Planning Commission, exist for at least the next twenty-five years. A residential area of twelve thousand people, Concord will grow to fifty thousand by 1995.

First Baptist Church, Concord has met this growth challenge by building new facilities, expanding the programs and staff of the church, making multiple use of buildings, and continuing to share her faith. One problem arose in 1974 when the church voted to go to two Sunday Schools. Good communication made the second vote a meaningful success.

Another good quality of the church is the willingness of the older members to let new people come in and share new ideas and leadership. As the old adage goes, "Nothing succeeds like success." Candid honesty and truth spoken in love can aid the church in moving on for Christ. This positive attitude has meant much to problem solving and ministry growth.

Laypersons in First Baptist Church have a high degree of dedication to Christ. This is a layperson's church with capable deacons, teachers, and leaders. Especially do we have a large number of men actively involved. There is a vision in the church that draws the members to prayer and the concerned sharing of their time and faith.

As pastor of a rural-urban church, I can say the task has been challenging, the work rewarding, and the growth in spirit and numbers stimulating.

Change does create tension and joy at the same time. We have learned that it requires both for real growth to transpire.

20.
Central Baptist Church
Richmond, Virginia
William D. Dietrich, Jr., Pastor

The author of this case study was born in Hopewell, Virginia, and is a graduate of Virginia Commonwealth University. Dietrich studied also at the Southern Baptist Theological Seminary, Louisville, Kentucky, and was awarded the Doctor of Ministry degree by Luther Rice Seminary. He and his wife, Alethia, are the parents of six children. He has been the pastor of Central Church since 1953.

From one decision made years ago, the history of Central Baptist Church begins.

Bethlehem Baptist Church was organized in 1792 and has had the honor of planting several new churches. In 1895 the church found its old building too far gone for repairs and the majority of the members agreed on a new house. With the decision to change the location of the new building, a split in the membership resulted. The group who did not leave started Spring Creek Baptist Mission in rural Chesterfield County.

On April 1, 1900, Spring Creek organized and adopted the name of Central Baptist Church. This congregation of twenty-five affiliated with the Southern Baptist Convention.

From conversations with older members about the first sanctuary, it seems the timber used in the building came from the farmlands of the charter members—cut, sawed and hauled by wagon to the site.

Land has always been important in our area. What were once rolling fields of wheat and corn and truck gardens are now subdivisions with thousands of people, all within a few minutes of our property which consists of twenty-four acres including the cemetery.

This land will prove to be an even greater asset as more subdivisions and roads are cut in the vicinity.

Our original building was an attractive but simple wood structure with steeple and some painted glass windows. In 1954, our Sunday School moved into a new building on the south side of our complex. The second major building program was in 1958 when the church adopted plans to build a new sanctuary. This meant, of course, tearing down a building which had served well for fifty-eight years. At the time we were having two worship services with Sunday School in between. Many were opposed to tearing down the "little white church on the hill." However, the final vote determined that rather than have the building moved and left to decay, it should be demolished and put to rest on the hill where it was born. The present sanctuary, seating approximately seven hundred people, stands in its place today.

In 1967, a children's building was planned to meet the needs of the community. That building is on the north side of the sanctuary. Facilities in the Sunday School today will accommodate about one thousand people.

The city of Richmond is surrounded by three counties, Henrico, Hanover, and Chesterfield. With the coming of the 1950s these were rapidly becoming bedroom communities. Men and women of all professions sought their livelihood in the city and the suburbs for home, social, and religious life.

Suddenly Central Baptist Church was no longer located on a dusty backroad. Surveyors were seen everywhere preparing to widen, straighten, and pave what had once been wagon trails. Large farms, where the members had once cut hay, threshed their wheat, and harvested their corn and pumpkins, became desirable locations for housing.

One subdivision of about fifty homes was developed less than a mile from us. Prospects appeared for the first time in years and evangelism became a reality.

I came to the church in 1953 and soon realized that there were possibilities far greater than anyone imagined for the future of the church.

We began to study such books as *A Church Using Its Sunday School, Teaching Adults in the Sunday School,* and *The Pull of the People.* We enlisted and trained Sunday School workers and developed a strong organization. This planning and training, coupled with a program of visitation, brought in the people and our Sunday School has been growing ever since.

Before long we had to go to two morning worship services, with the Sunday School hour coming between the two services. The interest of our congregation has increased not only in the Sunday School but in every phase of church-related work.

In 1953 we reported four baptisms. In 1957 we reported twenty. Our offerings grew from $8,360 in 1953 to $26,281 in 1957. Our mission offerings increased, and our huge building debt was being paid.

Also during this period, the church combined all weekly meetings of various church groups into one night with a fellowship supper. At the time, it was the only church in Chesterfield County undertaking this. It was not unusual in those days to have as many as 170 for supper and the prayer service.

Those years were years of excitement, challenge, and purpose. The little country church by the side of the road was taking on a completely new complexion.

The median age of the members in the 1950s was about sixty; however, each year as young couples moved into the community, the age of the church grew younger and younger. With the coming of "the new people," additional services and demands were constantly made on the church struggling to pay off a debt. Four years and three months after the dedication of the first unit, the debt was paid and plans were begun for a new sanctuary. The church minutes record that with all obligations paid to date, there remained only one penny in the treasury—and the church moved on!

Our members started exercising gifts which had not been apparent before moving into a modern building. We began to distinguish at least five characteristics of the people of God which have given us a clear sense of direction. They are:

1. **The church is a chosen people.** The emphasis here is on the fact of God's sovereignty and initiative; it is God who moves to choose and redeem a people for himself. The church is the result

of God's sovereignty and grace (2 Tim. 1:9).

2. The church is a pilgrim people. Here we have an emphasis which is difficult but biblically necessary—difficult, because it can be misconstrued to mean theological and practical withdrawal from the world, but necessary, because without this emphasis the church tends to slip into the worst kind of worldliness.

3. The church is a covenant people. The relationship between God and his people is specific and is morally and ethically based. The church is grounded in such a covenant understanding.

4. The church is a witness people. Its task is to point to that which has happened in the past and is happening in the present which is truly the action of God.

5. The church is a holy people. The biblical demand for holiness is insistent. Says Paul, Christ sanctifies the church that it may be "without spot or wrinkle or any such thing, that she might be holy and without blemish" (Eph. 5:27, RSV).

The year 1958 was the beginning of great change as far as Central church was concerned. The congregation had planned for several years to replace the frame structure which had served well for so long. Now it was no longer adequate for the needs of the community. The die was cast. Within a few weeks the session would be held which would decide the ministry of this old country church.

One man in the congregation was the recognized church patriarch. Brought as a young lad to Central by his parents, assisting in the actual building, growing up and serving in almost every official capacity the church could elect him to, he was a power to be reckoned with. I remember many meetings in which those present would first look to see how he was voting before they raised their hands. As in most churches this size, someone has to lead. Through those long years, Central had been fortunate to have this wise and dedicated layman to assist in leading.

How many people have said: "He runs the church." Well, after a fashion he did. He was a man of God and usually wise was his counsel. Yet, confrontation had to take place between this fine layman and me over the building of the new sanctuary.

The afternoon was warm (and it was to get warmer). "Brother

Dietrich," he began, "you've been our pastor five years. Many new people have come into the church. The spacious new education building is completed and paid for, and you are preaching twice on Sunday morning and once on Sunday evening. You've had a good ministry here at Central Church." . . . (Well, so far, so good, I thought . . .) "Now Brother Dietrich, I voted for you to come to this church and have appreciated your ministry. However, I've come here this afternoon to inform you that if you dare touch or allow anyone else to touch any part of that old building with the thought of tearing it down, you had better start looking for another pastorate. There are many more good years in that building and I can remember all that the old folks of Central did to erect it. Money was scarce, times were hard, we had no preacher; but we had a mind to work, and we did. Now a business meeting is coming up in two weeks and the matter will be settled then!" Having spoken his piece, my brother lit his pipe and went across the lawn to his automobile.

Talk about the church power structure. There it was all wrapped up in the form of a saint about seventy years of age. What to do? Where to go? Run scared? Preach out against such audacity from the pulpit? None of these.

You see, this man had two sons-in-law, young progressive builders and themselves rising in status. We all knew that the "old man of the church" did not have the influence he once had, but who among us wanted him to know that?

An old pastor in the Richmond area once said to me, "Son, never push the people of the church too fast or too far. Let them know the needs, share the needs with the Heavenly Father, then sit back and let the Holy Spirit run interference for you." I discovered that it works!

Another afternoon, same patriarch, same pastor, same problem; but the Holy Spirit had done his work. "Pastor," said he, "I'm here to tell you this afternoon that, next week, if the congregation votes to tear down the old building and erect a new sanctuary, I'll not stand in the way. I won't like it one bit, but if the majority votes to build, then you can count on me."

The church voted unanimously to tear down the old building and build a new house to the glory of God. Our patriarch served on the building committee. On Sunday, September 19, 1960, the congregation moved into the new sanctuary with a service of homecoming and dedication.

The church was whole, in fellowship, and began looking beyond its walls for the first time in its history. Oh, Central had supported various mission causes and was loyal to the denomination, but her eyes had been blinded to real mission needs. People were coming from all areas of the county to the new church. The gospel was being preached, the music was good, we were meeting in beautiful facilities, but the people continued to be content until we discovered a little book entitled, *New Testament Evangelism* by Hershel H. Hobbs. This small volume in group study was to make a difference in the vision of our people.

Growth was everywhere in the community and the church, but Central church was still dealing with rural-minded people. Older members had depended on cakewalks, pie sales, oyster suppers, and box parties to raise money when needed. Tithing was scriptural but not practical. We worked hard on such attitudes.

About this time, Bethlehem Baptist Church, together with the association, planted a mission only a few miles from Central. The reaction from our people? An item was placed at once in the budget to pay a monthly sum to this small congregation, and four laypersons from our congregation were sent to assist. Today that chapel is Lyndale Baptist Church, self-supporting and worshiping in a modern facility.

Adults were coming in great numbers to us and they brought their children. Neither could be relegated to the halls of the church buildings nor the damp basement of the parsonage. With keen insight for the future and complete faith, the third in our series of buildings was built. It was filled on the first Sunday.

The 1960s saw tremendous Sunday School and church growth. The people of the community saw a church willing to change for them, a church willing to sacrifice and build for them, a church willing to prepare for those not yet located in the community. We have given top priority to our Sunday School organization, especially since 1975, when we began purging our rolls of "dead wood." We emphasize solid Bible study and this past year we averaged five hundred people in Sunday School each week without any special promotional efforts.

Date	New Members	Members	Budget
1955	68	410	$ 14,580
1960	72	584	45,097
1965	60	730	58,050
1970	47	1,097	79,671
1975	92	1,162	136,424
1976	67	1,195	168,370
1977	76	1,243	172,152
1978	109	1,352	172,374

An innovation in our worship experiences has been the removal of our Sunday evening worship services from the beauty of the sanctuary and the sounds of the pipe organ. We go where our people are—in their neighborhoods.

From the beginning of June until Labor Day, our evening services are held in the yards of our members, in a different area each week. Led in music by our high school choir of forty to sixty voices accompanied on an electric piano, the congregation assembles in comfortable attire—perhaps having just returned from a family picnic, playing tennis, boating, etc. Bringing their folding chairs, they come for a forty-five minute service of praise.

The people of the neighborhood know we are coming through leaflets left neatly in their doors on the Saturday before. Attendance is usually up 300 to 400 percent over the services in the church sanctuary.

Despite these successful innovations, reappraisal of the commitment of the church continues to be necessary and vital. Will we remain the church of 1,350 members, gaining and losing the same number of members each year, static in offerings as well, or will we take a new look to determine needs?

Central church is now re-evaluating its ministries to the community and world missions. Many of the old systems have outlived their usefulness and we must become more optimistic about changes which may bring us further from our traditions but closer to the New Testament tradition of Jesus Christ. A long-range planning committee is at work and is being guided by definite objectives such as:

1. The committee is not to have pre-conceived ideas on what may or may not be needed at Central. Their work shall be one of exploring, seeking, and studying what is now required or may be needed in the future.

2. The committee is to announce all meetings and the meetings are to be open to all church members.

3. The committee is to develop and present to the members five-to-ten-year church objectives.

4. The committee is to try to develop several alternatives on all recommendations presented to the church.

5. The committee should be unanimous on the overall recommendations presented to the church.

6. The committee should remember that we are not working and expanding to keep up with other churches. We are working, planning, and expanding to meet God's requirements to teach and spread his Gospel to all people.

We are seeking a fellowship of people who though they recognize that they are inadequate, nevertheless can be personally involved in the effort to make Christ's kingdom prevail. Many of the members of Central are not involved at all and they do not even think it strange that they are not.

If the church is to prevail, if the message of Jesus Christ is to be heard, then these members must be motivated to understand the need for personal loyalty to Christ, sharing personally in the ministries of the church. Central church cannot allow itself to be constantly weakened by those who have some sort of connection with the church, but not one of involvement.

The county in which we are located will more than triple in

population during the next twenty-five years—from 123,500 to about 440,000. In the 1950s only one subdivision was within a five-mile radius of the church. There now are about thirty-five. Only three churches were in the community. Now there are fifteen.

No longer can the pastor or laity stand expectantly on the steps of the church to welcome the newcomer. People today search for the church of their choice—the one which can offer them more—and denominational lines are often crossed.

Paul sought to teach the congregation at Ephesus, "And these were his gifts: some to be . . . pastors and teachers, to equip God's people for work in his service" (Eph. 4:11-12, NEB).

The God-called pastor has nothing to fear from God-fearing, Spirit-filled men and women. They are the secret to church renewal.

The congregation of Jesus Christ meeting at Central Baptist Church, Richmond, Virginia, can be compared with the dreamer of the Old Testament, Joseph. He dreamed dreams and suffered because of them, but he did not fail! Enlistment, commitment, training, going, and telling will all become a greater part of our experience in the coming years.

Conclusion

Answers to the multitude of problems which confront the contemporary churches in urban areas do not come quickly or easily. Neither are there any foolproof methods to use in responding fully to the myriad opportunities for Christian ministry surrounding these churches. Such a ministry calls mainly for a deep conviction of being in the will of God, plenty of hard work, creative imagination, an abundance of faith, a love for people, and a desire to glorify Jesus Christ as Lord and Savior.

Personal involvement in a church in a changing community is difficult at best. Quite often one is inclined to utter a prayer similar to the meditation of the late Dean of the Harvard Divinity School, Samuel H. Miller: [6]

Walk with us, O God, in the plain paths where the day by day routine settles down to a test of private perseverance, unheralded by the accolade of praise or bright reward. If the heavenly vision grows dim, and our hearts are weary in well doing, lay thy hand upon us and steady our steps that we may press onward, even in darkness, toward the light ahead. If we are alone, and the task seems more than we can do, or if done, not at all welcomed by the world, reveal thy presence at our side that we may labor with thy help. Turn us from the dreams of far glory to work in the commonplace circumstances of this mortal world, and disclose to us the miracle of thy grace in unexpected places. Even so may thy will be done on earth as it is in heaven, through Jesus Christ our Lord. Amen.

The churches discussed in these case studies are noteworthy indeed, in the ways they have dealt with community change. They are still on their journey, but they are fine models of present-day discipleship. They are representative of numerous congregations over the land that are equally as fine at facing change, but they are also worthy examples for other churches in similar situations which are struggling with self-identity and meaningful action.

These twenty churches see the necessity for maintaining a servant posture in urban America. Some of them are gritty churches, having faced extinction but opted for a daring, aggressive ministry in the name of Christ. They possess an evangelistic compassion for people of all races and conditions in the context of human need. They are not pursuing eccentric tangents or erecting ego-pleasing monuments. Instead, they have faced and are facing social change with a positive, constructive attitude.

Each case study could have been much longer in order to include all of the activities of the churches. However, the descriptions given present a careful analysis of the churches as both the strengths and the weaknesses are discussed.

It is interesting to note that the churches have many similarities. For instance, congregations in central city and inner city neighborhoods have trouble accepting newcomers, especially if the new people are different socially or racially from the members. Churches in suburban and rural-urban fringe areas have the same trouble. Change, particularly if it is rapid, is troublesome to deal with in any location. Churches do well to learn from one another in order to strengthen their effectiveness in coping with transition.

Often young churches begin with a small homogeneous group and become more culturally and racially inclusive as the years pass and communities change. Those churches which deliberately avoid such diversity may experience neighborhood isolation after a while and be forced to remove themselves from a vibrant Christian ministry.

It has been demonstrated frequently that a church which is truly seeking to reach people over a span of time will include in its fellowship a percentage of persons representative of the community. That is, if the area is 70 percent white, 10 percent black, and 20 percent Oriental, the membership of the church will often reveal similar percentages. If the community has in it factory workers, teachers, farmers, students, businessmen, and retired persons, the church will include practically the same types of people at nearly the same percentages.

That the urban centers of the nation are in rapid transition is an established fact. Blacks are moving to the suburbs, while ethnics and whites are quietly easing into the cities. At the same time small tracts of land in exurbia are being purchased by new homeowners at a fast pace.

For many individuals the changing communities provide an improved way of life, because some neighborhoods offer better housing and living conditions than those people have experienced previously. Scores of families are in fact, now celebrating their new communities which is a factor often overlooked.

It is becoming apparent that a predominate WASP culture is disappearing in America as families from other countries arrive. No longer is the "melting pot" theory of assimilation practical because so many minority groups prefer to retain their cultural identities. Yet the United States is more than a "mosaic" of races and cultures with each one being distinct and separate. That which is emerging is somewhere between the "melting pot" and the "mosaic" as more and more people of different backgrounds give and receive from each other on a daily basis.

Churches serving with grace and fidelity in an urban society need more than ever to start with people where they are, meeting their needs without being paternalistic, and involving them in the full work of the congregation. Open pluralism is becoming increasingly the style of life for metropolitan churches and should remain so for decades to come.

Implications for Pastors

These case studies indicate once again that the leadership of the pastor is indispensable. Many times the church will rise or fall on the vision, the skills, the faith, and the integrity of the pastor. To be a pastor is an awesome calling, for the pastor, striving for reconciliation, has the responsibility of standing in the gap between wayward human beings and a forgiving God.

Contemporary mankind, greatly secularized, is lonely and seeking fulfillment. Personal relationships are often shallow and temporary. Millions of our citizens are in a hurry, but going nowhere. Without leadership, many are lost.

I recently heard a respected Christian layman reflecting on the Old Testament character, Joshua. He suggested that if God had not produced for the beleaguered Hebrews, an astute, trustworthy leader like Joshua, they may not have made it to the promised land at all! This layman was discussing the constant need of the church for the leadership function of the pastor.

It is my understanding that an Israeli officer never says to his troops, "Charge." Instead, he shouts, "Follow me."

Without question the New Testament instructs the pastor to equip the church members for ministry (Eph. 4:11-15). However, the pastor must be careful to avoid believing that his only duty is to coach the people and then stay on the sidelines or in the background. Modern lives require more than that, and power-hungry cultists and money-grabbing quack preachers who play on personal fears of heaven or hell know it.

Churches in changing communities need leadership of the finest caliber. The pastors must be not only equippers but also leaders on the front lines of battle. Some pastors make the mistake of training their people for ministry but never leading them to do ministry. When this happens, the pastor waits on the parishioners to act, and the parishioners wait on the pastor to lead them. The result is lethargy and scapegoatism. The pastor is the one in the position to initiate an affirmative strategy so that the church can move forward in Christian ministry. It is the pastor's responsibility to do so.

Implications for Laity

The leadership potential of the pastor quite often resides with the parishioners. That is, if they dogmatically desire to keep the Good News of Jesus Christ to themselves and refuse to reach out to new people through evangelism and missions, the pastor's leadership is voided. If a pastor is successful in his work, it usually means

that the laity of the church are outstanding in their commitment
to Christ.

No one encourages the pastor like lay persons, but the opposite
also is true as no one discourages pastors like the laity. It may be
that the primary function of church members is to be wide-awake
encouragers in the spirit and fashion of Barnabas.

It does not need to be emphasized that the pastor cannot do
the work of the church by himself. To even try such would be in
violation of New Testament principles and personally devastating.
The more the pastor and parishioners serve together, the more the
church will progress in building up the kingdom of God.

It has been said that "happiness is the by-product of a meaningful
life." Few churches offer a more fertile ground for a meaningful,
purposeful life than do those churches located in transitional communities. As opportunities abound for sharing (which is always more
blessed than receiving), in churches where social and racial changes
are occurring, pastor and people discover regularly that their lives
are enriched as they serve others.

Implications for Seminaries

It was extremely interesting to study the case studies in regards
to planning. Practically every church engaged in short, medium,
and long-range planning. Some planned their work better than others
and have been doing so over a longer period of time. Several of
the churches entered into serious planning willingly and eagerly,
while others hesitated. A few refused to plan their ministries and
activities until they were forced to do so by the community changes
which exploded around them.

This should say something to our seminaries. In addition to equipping future ministers in such necessary disciplines as theology, pastoral psychology, homiletics, and church history, the seminaries might
do well to take a closer look at modern society. We are in a social
revolution in America. From one corner of the nation to another,
upheaval is taking place and it has been happening for almost two
decades with the end not yet in sight. Particularly is this the situation
in metropolitan areas. If we aren't careful the revolution may pass

by scores of seminaries and churches which elect to turn away from realism.

More than at any time in the past, church leaders must be skilled in planning techniques and methods. Too much is happening too fast. Political, economic, racial, personal rights, and birth-rate trends need to be studied by churches in preparation for sharing the Gospel. Educational, family, and moral trends beg to be taken into account.

If the seminaries are serious about producing graduates who will be able to "rightly divide the word of truth" in a rapidly changing country, major attention must be given to helping the students understand and make use of planning processes and procedures. Society is going to require it more and more and churches, especially in urban centers, are going to expect it from their pastors. Alternatives to planning are becoming fewer all the time.

Our seminaries would do well also, in light of current conditions, to seek hastily for students, faculty members, and administrators from minority ranks.

Implications for Denominations

Perhaps the most noticeable weakness of the churches in the case studies has to do with an ignoring of power groups in society who determine constructive or destructive policies which affect so many citizens. Thousands of churches in America do the same. Rarely do church leaders come to realize that what is taking place in their community is the direct result of decisions being made at city hall, or by the county commissioners, or at financial institutions. Often those decisions are made for selfish gains without regard for the ultimate welfare of the community, and churches seldom question what is being done.

It most likely is true that the average pastor in America is a decent, hard-working, caring individual; but his one biggest sin is that he is too quiet. He neglects to speak out against injustice in high places. If the pastor is silent, how can the church do otherwise? There are exceptions, of course, in a few of the case studies.

Denominational officials can help pastors and churches in such circumstances by calling attention to needs, corruption, and unfairness through training conferences, publications, speeches, and confrontation. Often a denominational group can open closed doors much quicker and with less pain than a local congregation can. In doing so the denominational leaders become sources of inspiration and courage for local church leaders caught up in radical change.

The persistent need exists as well for denominational strategists to always keep in focus that older churches should be strengthened even as new churches are being started. It is not an either/or matter. At the same time the agencies of the denominations can help by enabling churches to identify specific points of community transition along with a follow-through plan of action. As societal change continues to transpire in the years ahead, more model churches and individual leaders will need to emerge. There is no question about the blessing which would come to the cities of America if thousands of our organized churches would engage in the kinds of ministries which are sorely needed. Hopefully we will be found faithful.

Notes

1. Henri J. M. Nouwen, *Reaching Out* (New York: Doubleday & Company, Inc., 1975), p. 46.

2. Ibid., pp. 50-51.

3. "On Hospitality," *The Catholic Worker*, May 1976, pp. 5, 11.

4. Worley, Robert C. *Dry Bones Breathe* (Chicago: Center for the Study of Church Organizational Behavior, 1978), p. 14.

5. Worley, Robert C., *Change in the Church: A Source of Hope* (Philadelphia: Westminster Press, 1971), p. 95.

6. Samuel H. Miller, *Prayers for Daily Use* (New York: Harper and Row Publishers, 1957), p. 15.